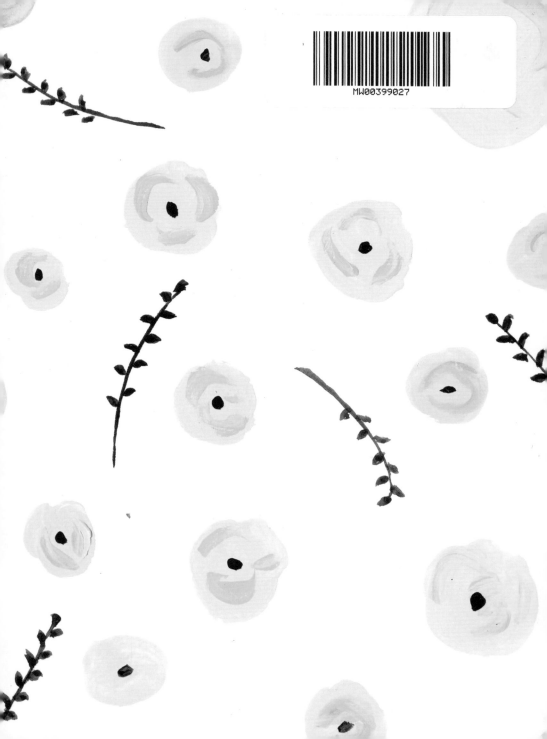

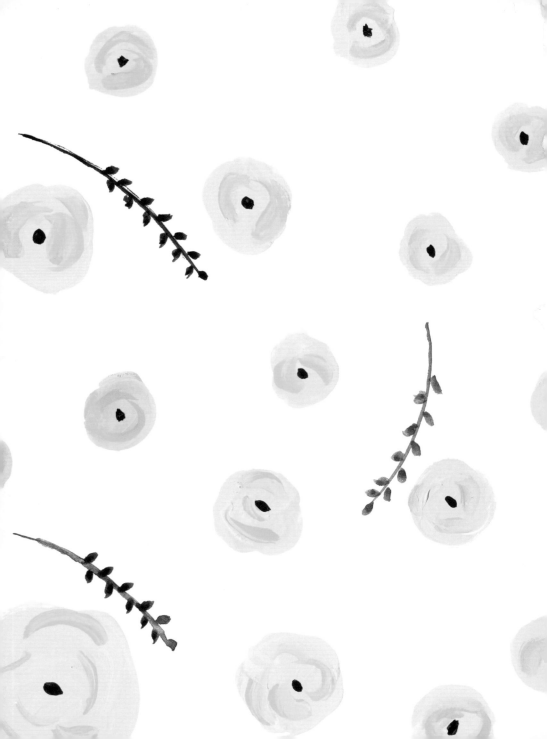

To:

....

From:

....

Find Rest

Best-Selling Author of *For Women Only*
SHAUNTI FELDHAHN

Foreword by
Nancy DeMoss Wolgemuth

Christian art gifts®

Visit Christian Art Gifts, Inc. at www.christianartgifts.com.

Find Rest

Published by Christian Art Gifts, Inc., under license from iDisciple LLC.

Cover and interior images used under license from Shutterstock.com

Cover designed by Nicole Grimes.

Requests for information should be addressed to: iDisciple, 2555 Northwinds Parkway, Alpharetta, GA 30009

ISBN 978-1-64272-153-9   GB180
ISBN 978-1-63952-409-9   GB257

Printed in China

28 27 26 25 24 23
10 9 8 7 6 5 4 3 2 1

Foreword

Overcommitted and overwhelmed.
Hurried and harried.
Racing at warp speed and running on empty.
Out of breath and on edge.
Can't keep up and can't slow down.
Expended and exhausted.
Wrung out and worn out.
Depleted and defeated.
Stretched and stressed.
Anxious and restless.

Sound familiar?

This is what I often sense when I look into the eyes and hearts of my Christian sisters.

All too often, it's what I see when I slow down long enough to consider what's going on in my own soul.

And based on what Shaunti has written in these sixty short devotional readings, I'd say she's no stranger to this same breathless-on-the-treadmill-of-life sort of experience.

Yet she understands, and she wants us to understand, that the gospel (and this is Good News indeed) calls us to another way.

God's Word promises us green pastures and still waters, times of refreshing rivers of living water flowing from within.

So from one needy pilgrim to another, I invite you to push pause, step into these pages, let your mind be renewed, and let your racing heart slow down.

Mostly I invite you come to Christ. And in Him, find:

Grace and gratitude.
Contentment and courage.
Peace and perspective.
Dependence and delight.
Trust and thriving.
Strength and sanity.
A slower pulse and steady praise.
Worship and wonder.
Restoration and refreshing.
In a word, rest.

Our Savior beckons to you and to me:
"Stand by the roads, and look,
and ask for the ancient paths,
where the good way is; and walk in it,
and find rest for your souls."
— Jeremiah 6:16

Stop your running, He says. Stand still. Look at the way you're heading. Ask for directions to a new and different place (actually an ancient place). Walk in that good way—His way, the paths walked by those who have gone before us. Find rest for your soul.

— Nancy DeMoss Wolgemuth

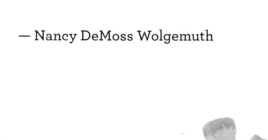

A Personal Note

Friends, this devotional is going to take us on a personal journey to find true rest.

I call you friends because I feel like I know you. We share the common bond of being sisters in Christ and being women who spend a lot of time running. We may be as different as can be—single or married, a senior executive or a stay-at-home mom, a newlywed or an empty nester—but we all know the feeling of bouncing around like we're in a pinball game. I know I sure do.

Ziiinng! Time to get up and make lunches, get myself ready, and hustle the kids out the door for school. *Zoiinnng!* Oh no, I'm running late for that big meeting, and traffic is horrible! *Zaaaapp!* The project isn't working right, my daughter is sick, I didn't meet that school deadline, and I'm worried about disappointing my colleague, friend, sister-in-law, or volunteer coordinator. *Zooom!* Time to rush my son to his guitar lesson, work on my laptop in the parking lot, check in with my husband (have I even talked to him today?), call a friend to vent, and figure out dinner before running out to women's Bible study or the volleyball game. *Zonk.* The ball stopped bouncing. It hit a wall and so did I. I may snap at someone (or myself!), get discouraged about having to work late, or simply fall into exhausted sleep the moment my head hits the pillow.

Any of this sound familiar?

Some days we handle the emotional and physical juggling act well. Some days we really need a do-over. Either way, it rarely feels like we find true rest.

Friends, look at these precious words of Jesus:

"Come to me, all of you who are weary and carry heavy burdens, and I will give you rest. Take my yoke upon you. Let me teach you, because

I am humble and gentle at heart, and you will find rest for your souls." (Matthew 11:28-29)

This is a promise. There is a way to find rest. It will not always be rest in our bodies, with the many demands that come with being the women we're called to be. But it will be rest in our souls. We can experience a life of peace and joy amidst the storms.

It almost feels impossible—but it's not.

Since I'm both a follower of Christ and a researcher, I've been studying both what the Bible says and what science says about this. I've found that so much of the stress and worry we face doesn't have to be there! Much of our stress comes from missing a few key truths, not realizing the importance of a different mind-set or different actions, or not trusting the promises of a God whose mercies are new every morning. I've compiled those essential elements into a series of themes and topics that we will consider in daily devotional times with the Lord. (See the *Elements of Finding Rest* on page vi.)

In other words, this devotional is more than just a "time out" or a moment of peace in a beautiful garden of inspiration each day. It is a series of simple but crucial moments that, if you truly enter in to them, will lead you to find rest in your "inner soul"—a place of true, Christ-centered peace, no matter where the daily pinball game sends you.

And that peace—the peace God offers—will give you delight in this crazy, wonderful life you are living, in a way that overflows onto all those around you.

See you in the garden, friends.

— Shaunti Feldhahn

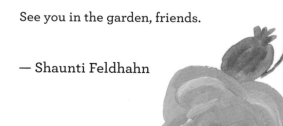

Elements of Finding Rest

- Build Only on Rock

- Live According to Your Design

- Set Aside Superwoman

- Connect with God

- Shift Your Perspective

- Create Life-Giving Relationships

- Walk in Obedience

- Have No Fear

*Thus says the LORD: "Stand by the roads, and
look, and ask for the ancient paths, where the good
way is; and walk in it, and find rest for your souls."*
— Jeremiah 6:16, ESV

Finding Your Good Way

When I moved to New York City in 1994, I spent a lot of time on the subway. Always busy, I enjoyed speeding under the gridlocked traffic to quickly reach my destination. Most of Manhattan is laid out in a clear grid pattern with numbered streets, so getting around is easy.

As long as you know where you are, you know exactly where to go. I'm at 32nd and Park, so I just need to head north two blocks and turn right on 34th street.

There is just one hitch: When you come off the subway at an unfamiliar stop, how do you know where you are? Surrounded by tall buildings, you have no sense of direction.

In those days, there was an easy solution: we would turn in a circle until we spotted the Twin Towers, which were clearly visible at the southern tip of Manhattan. We knew that was south, so we could use that landmark to determine where we were and where to go. We based our sense of direction on the Twin Towers because they were fixed and unmoving.

Until they weren't. On September 11, 2001, every New Yorker—and

every person on the planet, really—saw the truth that all man-made things are temporary.

In our crazy, modern lives, each of us is looking for direction: how do we get to that life of peace and joy we want, rather than the stressed and frazzled life we have? All too often, we base our decisions on things that loom large in our eyes—convenience, the advice of friends, whether it avoids pain or brings pleasure. But those factors are a fickle guide.

We are stressed and frazzled because we have followed temporary directional signals that do not lead to peace (the "good way," as the prophet Jeremiah put it).

Jesus quoted the prophet Jeremiah when he said there is only one way to find that good way: taking on His yoke and learning from Him. (Matthew 11:29).

We must stop looking to temporary signals for a sense of direction. We must look to the One who both never changes and is gentle with our human, frazzled state. As we will see on Day 2, His yoke (guiding force) will never pull us astray.

Reflect

Think of a decision (small or large) that is causing you stress, that you need to make in the coming days. What temporary things might you be looking to for a sense of direction? (For example, the path of least resistance at the moment, or what your colleagues are suggesting you do...) What unchanging truth can you look to instead?

Notes

_____

_____

_____

_____

_____

_____

_____

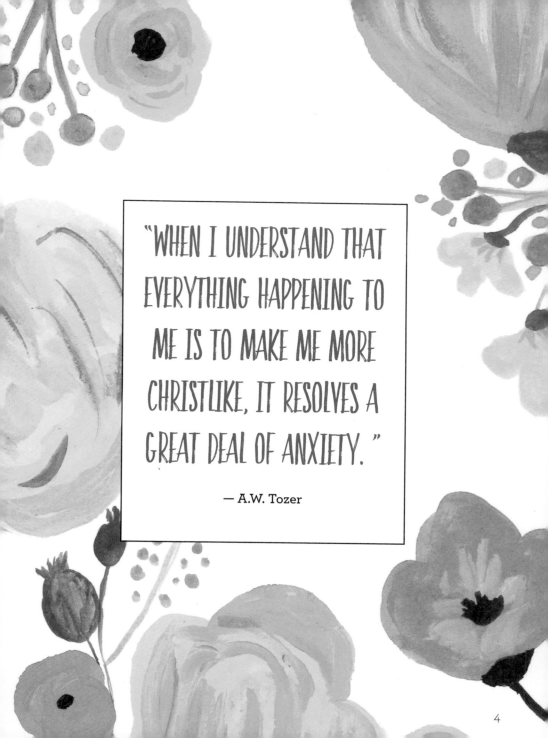

"WHEN I UNDERSTAND THAT EVERYTHING HAPPENING TO ME IS TO MAKE ME MORE CHRISTLIKE, IT RESOLVES A GREAT DEAL OF ANXIETY."

— A.W. Tozer

4

Come to me, all you who are weary and burdened, and I will give you rest. Take my yoke upon you and learn from me, for I am gentle and humble in heart, and you will find rest for your souls.
— Matthew 11:28-29, NIV

His Yoke Is Custom-Fit for You

When my children were small, money was very tight. The local annual consignment sales were a lifesaver for inexpensively outfitting two quickly-growing kids. I generally bought a size or two ahead so the kids had room to grow for the next year.

I thought the kids looked adorable in their oversized shirts and rolled-up jeans, but they were definitely not custom fit! I was asking them to live, play, and work in clothes that were not tailored to them in any way.

God is not like that. When Jesus says that a key way to find rest is to "Take my yoke upon you," He is gently rebuking us for taking on burdens that we were not meant to carry, and telling us to instead take on those purposes that He has created just for us.

A yoke is a device that hitches over the shoulders of a working animal (or team of animals) so they can comfortably pull something heavy, such as a plow. Since every animal is a different size and shape, a caring farmer carefully custom fits a yoke to each beast. This allows the ox or horse or donkey to work well when he is called upon, without getting exhausted, being ineffective from pulling at a wrong angle, or getting chafed and sore.

The farmer is also careful not to give a young animal a yoke that is too large. Instead, at every stage of growth, the farmer remeasures the beasts under his care and creates a new yoke. The animal is called to a particular purpose, and he is outfitted for it.

Imagine the difficulty if one animal were to take on the yoke that was designed for another. The ground might get plowed, but oh the pain and strain and heaviness! Oh, the open sores on a weary back! After days and months of this, wouldn't the animal eventually shy away from the good work of the day?

So often, we are weary and burdened not because of long hours or having too much to do, but because we are taking on things we were never meant to do, or in a way or during a time we were never meant to do them. Let us believe our Lord's promise that when we take up His yoke for us, we will find rest.

Reflect

What are you taking on that may not be God's fit or design for you? How can you set that aside and avoid that temptation in the future?

Notes

_____

_____

_____

_____

_____

_____

_____

_____

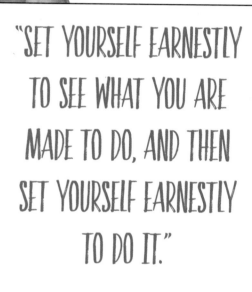

"SET YOURSELF EARNESTLY
TO SEE WHAT YOU ARE
MADE TO DO, AND THEN
SET YOURSELF EARNESTLY
TO DO IT."

— Phillips Brooks

Day 3

It is useless for you to work so hard from early morning until late at night, anxiously working for food to eat; for God gives rest to his loved ones.
— *Psalm 127:2*

No More Superwoman!

Our society is tired. Dog tired. And women, specifically, seem to be the most tired of all. That's why we are tempted by the latest and greatest pill, potion, powder, or diet that will give us more energy.

Exhaustion has become the social norm amongst busy women. And let's admit the hard truth: We often find ourselves glorifying the busy schedules, giving ourselves a pat on the back when we squeeze one more commitment into an already too-packed day and admiring others who seem to handle the juggling act as if they were a professional in a three-ring circus.

Even crazier, we also tend to consider ourselves lazy if we want a break from our busy schedules. What am I doing sitting and reading a book for half an hour over lunch? I signed up to make party favors for the teacher appreciation event, and I have to turn in that report on the Boston merger tomorrow, and I need to clean the house before the dinner party tomorrow night!

As we push ourselves beyond what we were designed to bear, we also overlook the physical and emotional signs that we're doing too much. We rush at breakneck speed right into stress that God never intended us to bear. Remember? He gives rest to His loved ones.

Set Aside Superwoman

There are basic elements of self-care—diet, exercise, and sleep—that will help create balance in our lives. We need to do those things. But they don't solve the chronic problem. We have a bone-deep exhaustion because we are trying to be Superwoman. We have bought into the lie that we can have it all, do it all, and be it all—all at the same time.

We were not designed for that. We were designed to have to make choices. To prioritize. To realize that above a certain threshold, which is a whole lot lower than we like to think, every extra good thing we take on is a net negative for us and for God's purposes for our lives. We were not designed to be Superwomen. If we want to be in charge of teacher appreciation, that means being okay with warmly welcoming our guests the following night into a somewhat messy but loving home, populated by people who understand the art of putting their attention where it really matters.

Reflect

How might you be trying to have it all, all at the same time? How is that affecting you, and what is one thing you can do to change it?

Notes

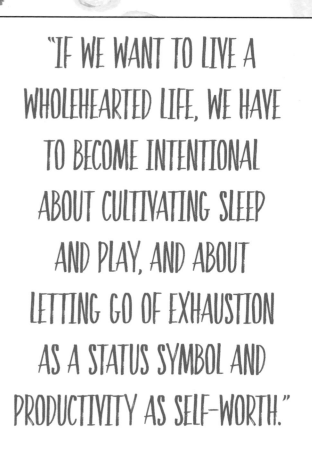

"IF WE WANT TO LIVE A WHOLEHEARTED LIFE, WE HAVE TO BECOME INTENTIONAL ABOUT CULTIVATING SLEEP AND PLAY, AND ABOUT LETTING GO OF EXHAUSTION AS A STATUS SYMBOL AND PRODUCTIVITY AS SELF-WORTH."

— Brené Brown
The Gifts Of Imperfection

12

Do you not know? Have you not heard? The Lord is the everlasting God, the Creator of the ends of the earth. He will not grow tired or weary, and his understanding no one can fathom. He gives strength to the weary and increases the power of the weak.
— *Isaiah 40:28-29, NIV*

Plug into Your Source of Strength

We've all been there—our phone battery suddenly drops into the red zone just when an important call comes in. Will the battery hold out? Or will it go dead, leaving us sounding unprofessional? Or uncaring? Or simply unable to finish the important coordination with the home health aides who are checking on our elderly parents?

Finally we get to a place where we see a charger and outlet. We can breathe again as we continue the conversation, our battery power slowly creeping back up into the normal zone.

As women, our batteries often run dangerously low. We may try to plug into superficial power, such as an extra shot of espresso in the morning or some online shopping. Perhaps we rely on our friends to give us that boost to make us feel important and needed. Or we look to a boyfriend to fill the deep desire for love and affirmation.

But these power sources don't cut it. They can't quite get our battery to a full charge. We're left feeling frustrated, run down, let down, and even defeated.

There is only one real energy source, and it is not found at the coffee shop. It is found in that moment when we come before the One who understands every minute detail about us and longs to give power to those who know they are weary and weak before Him.

You may feel like you need a nap, but He never grows weary. You may feel weak in the knees as you struggle to understand how to handle a difficult relationship, but He gives you strength. He provides guidance and wisdom and fills every single need of your heart. His charge will take hold and fill you. But here's the catch: You need to plug into Him.

Maybe that means adding time with God to your calendar every morning or joining a Bible study in order to read Scripture in a fresh way. Maybe it means listening to a sermon podcast while you make dinner or reaching out to a friend as an accountability partner who will remind you of the only true source of strength—God Himself.

Whatever method you try, it will make a dramatic difference in your life. God may not remove the circumstances that fill up your day, but He will give you the strength to walk with Him through it.

Reflect

In what way will you regularly plug into God's power going forward?

Notes

_____

_____

_____

_____

_____

_____

_____

_____

"WE NEED TO FIND GOD, AND HE CANNOT BE FOUND IN NOISE AND RESTLESSNESS. GOD IS THE FRIEND OF SILENCE ... WE NEED SILENCE TO BE ABLE TO TOUCH SOULS."

— Mother Teresa

Whatever is true, whatever is noble, whatever is right, whatever is pure, whatever is lovely, whatever is admirable—if anything is excellent or praiseworthy—think about such things.
— *Philippians 4:8, NIV*

What You Focus on Is What You'll See

In the classic "Invisible Gorilla" experiment video, created by Harvard University in 1999, six people in black and white shirts pass basketballs back and forth. A voice asks the viewer to count how many times the people in white shirts pass the basketball.

Simple, right?

Half of those who watch the video miss something very, very obvious—a gorilla. Yes, someone in a gorilla suit actually walks through the basketball passers, very clearly faces the camera and thumps his chest, and then walks offscreen. Half of us are so busy counting the passes between the white-shirted people that we never even notice it. When the video asks, "Did you see the gorilla?" we think, *Wait, what gorilla?!*

What we focus on will change what we observe around us. We will notice more and more of what we focus on or, conversely, less and less of what we don't want to see.

In the research for my book *The Kindness Challenge,* I found that this is one of the main reasons for the unneeded stress in our lives, and

one of the God-given ways to overcome it. As we focus on the things that annoy or anger us, well, you guessed it, we often completely miss some good and wonderful stuff that could change how we feel. We miss the gorilla! So often, when we are worried about our struggling marriage, frustrations with an adult child, a roommate's messiness, or our mean coworker, that negative thing looms large in our eyes. We think about it, ponder it, express frustration about it. And we never even see the other spectacular things going on around us.

Yet, as we focus on "whatever is lovely"—those good and true things we like and appreciate—we'll find ourselves noticing those things more often. And as we do, our negative concerns won't loom as large.

Suppose that instead of asking why your husband loaded the dishwasher that way (again!), you give him a hug and thank him for cleaning up the kitchen. What will happen to your feelings? You'll feel better! And as you look for the next thing to praise . . . and the next . . . you'll find that you don't really even notice what annoyed you so much before. Instead, you'll start noticing everything you can be grateful for.

It's a shift in focus that God asks us to make because He knows it delivers a big impact.

Reflect

What three positive "gorillas" are you missing
because other worries are looming too large
in your eyes? How can you change that?

Notes

_____

_____

_____

_____

_____

_____

_____

_____

"NEVER LOSE AN OPPORTUNITY
OF SEEING ANYTHING
BEAUTIFUL, FOR BEAUTY IS
GOD'S HANDWRITING."

— Ralph Waldo Emerson

*Every day they continued to meet together in the temple courts.
They broke bread in their homes and ate together with glad and
sincere hearts, praising God and enjoying the favor of all the people.*
— Acts 2:46-47, NIV

Created for Community

We were not created to do life alone. God looked at His creation and said "it is good," with one exception: it was absolutely not good for man to be alone. So God made someone with whom he could "do life." Then, in the first ever small group, God Himself walked in the garden with the man and his wife. Over and over in the Bible, God stresses that He designed us to love and support each other. We are directed (not asked) to live in community with other followers of Christ.

When I was living in Boston, a pastor shared a story about good friends who had moved to California. One night the pastor and his wife were awakened at 3 a.m. with an urgent phone call from their friends, asking for prayer. Raging wildfires were threatening their home and community. From their window, they could see the glow of thousands of acres burning, the fire advancing quickly as they raced to evacuate their home. The pastor and his wife got out of bed and knelt on the cold floor, praying urgently for an hour for the protection of their friends, their home, and everyone in the area.

In the end, although the fire consumed thousands of acres and several neighborhoods, the broader community—and their friends' house— was spared.

The homeowner called the pastor and thanked him profusely for being a true friend. The pastor answered, "No, thank you. You were the one being a true friend. You thought enough of our friendship that you were willing to wake us up in the middle of the night to ask us to pray. You were good enough friends that you were willing to 'inconvenience' us."

Our lives can be consumed by wildfires—personal family struggles, having too much on our plates, difficulties managing our kids or careers, health concerns, and financial strains. We can see the fires on the horizon, advancing toward us, and our chest tightens as life comes at us so fast. But God has created community for us to call on— even in the middle of the night. Are you willing to inconvenience a fellow believer in order to live in authentic community? That is what God has designed for you. And your willingness to do so will be a blessing to you both.

Reflect

How could you be more engaged in Christian community, including being willing to ask for help? How might that help you find rest?

Notes

_____

_____

_____

_____

_____

_____

_____

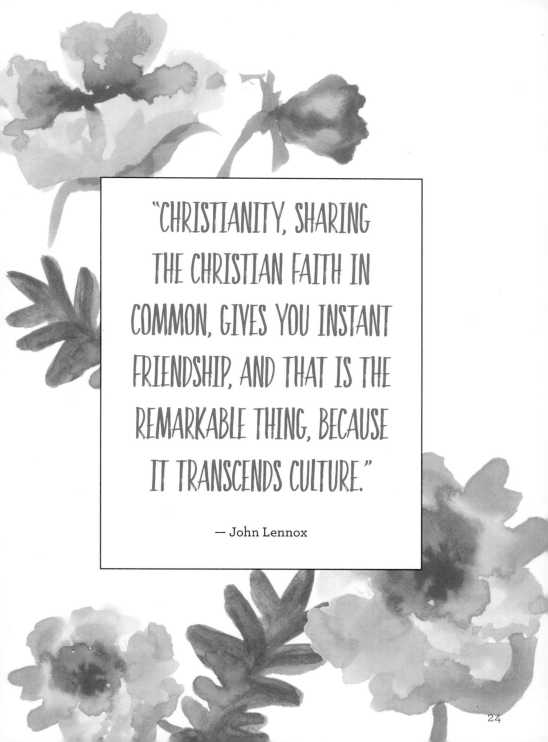

"CHRISTIANITY, SHARING THE CHRISTIAN FAITH IN COMMON, GIVES YOU INSTANT FRIENDSHIP, AND THAT IS THE REMARKABLE THING, BECAUSE IT TRANSCENDS CULTURE."

— John Lennox

So prepare your minds for action and exercise self-control.
Put all your hope in the gracious salvation that will come to
you when Jesus Christ is revealed to the world. So you must
live as God's obedient children. Don't slip back into your
old ways of living to satisfy your own desires. . . . You must be
holy in everything you do, just as God who chose you is holy.
— *1 Peter 1:13-15*

Self-Control and Self-Consequences

If you are a parent, one of your greatest callings (and challenges!) is teaching your children self-control. "Yes, I know you wanted to hit your sister, but you have to stop yourself. You can't just hit someone because you feel like it." "Sure, your brother/friend/classmate tried to provoke you, but that doesn't mean you say mean things back. Make a good choice, honey." "Don't roll your eyes at me, young lady." (Okay, I had to add that one.)

A child experiences stress and heartache when they live to satisfy their own desires. Their friends won't play with them. They feel guilt for being mean. They are punished for their actions. In the end, they get hurt even more. This stress is the direct consequence for doing what God does not intend.

It's easy to see the consequences for failing to live God's way in our children, but sometimes we miss them in our own lives.

After college, I certainly didn't connect my stress and anxiety with my holiness compromises. I was a brand-new follower of Christ, and yet I wasn't satisfied with His love and the love of many wonderful

new believing friends. I also wanted a boyfriend—someone to love me whether or not he was God's best for me, and whether or not I compromised God's standards in the process.

I intentionally hid the nature of my relationship from my Christian friends, knowing they would press me toward holiness. I knew perfectly well that I was being disobedient, and I did it anyway. It took quite some time for me to realize that the fights with my boyfriend, my distance from God, the conflict with friends, and my unusual level of exhaustion and stress at work were all (directly or indirectly) ramifications of that choice. Ramifications allowed by a God who was using pain to wake me up.

Friends, we have to confront the reality that sometimes the problems in our lives do not come because "we're living in a broken world," or "the enemy is attacking us." Sometimes our problems are a direct result of us failing to exercise self-control. We are not living in obedience. Just as we, as loving parents, will not let our children compromise without consequences, neither will our loving heavenly Father. He is calling us back to a path that will bring peace.

Reflect

If you are honest with yourself, in what ways are you satisfying
your own desires and not living up to God's standards of
holiness? Pray now, repenting of your disobedience and
asking God to help you change. Then commit to God and
to a close friend that you will walk in holiness from now on.

Notes

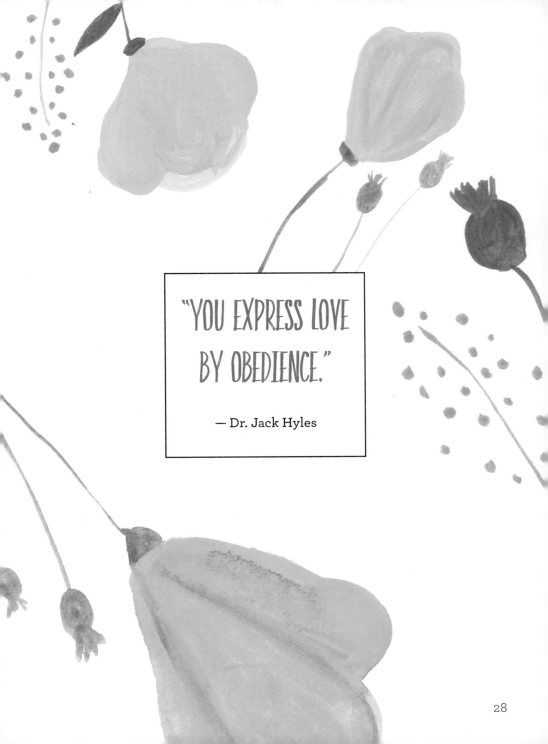

"YOU EXPRESS LOVE
BY OBEDIENCE."

— Dr. Jack Hyles

In this world you will have trouble. But
take heart! I have overcome the world.
— John 16:33, NIV

Knowing the End of the Story

Have you ever known someone who reads the last few pages of a book before they start the beginning of the book? One friend of mine reads the ending of every book first. It puts her mind at ease to know how the story will end—whether it's happy or sad and who lives or dies. This habit always seemed funny to me, since knowing the ending takes all the tension out of the intense chapters. At least I thought it was a funny habit, until I was reading one particular book and literally begged a friend to tell me what happened next. I needed reassurance that the story would turn out right in the end.

Our lives are a story. As we scroll through, page by page, some chapters are victorious, while others are full of struggle. Some are a bit mundane, but others contain milestones such as marriage, the birth of a child or grandchild, a big move, or a new job. Some are scary: that day we got a diagnosis or a loved one died.

Our stories are woven with many threads, including joy, worry, struggle, happiness, and—since we can't know what will happen tomorrow—the great unknown.

But what if we knew the ending? Would that change how we read the suspenseful chapter that we're in right now? How would we interpret those few pages that were filled with sadness or struggle?

As Christ followers, we do know the ending of our story. Jesus Himself tells us the plot: we will have trouble in this world, but He has overcome the world! There will be chapters of pain and heartbreak because we live in a big, broken, messy world. But then He flips to the last chapter because He wants us to know that in the end, He will defeat everything that makes us sad, scared, or defeated. We can't see eternity yet, but we can cling to the truth that once and for all, God does win against the enemy. And as children of God, we win too.

What is worrying you today? What dark threads of fear are trying to weave their way into your story? Trouble may be there, but fear doesn't have to be. In intense times, remind yourself that you know the ultimate ending. For those who are followers of Jesus, He promises us that the last chapter of our story is well worth it.

Reflect

How does your view of the current chapter of your life change when you remember that Jesus told you to take heart because He has overcome the world?

Notes

_____

_____

_____

_____

_____

_____

_____

_____

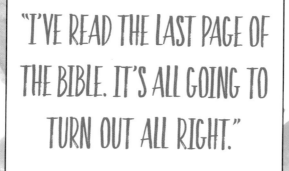

"I'VE READ THE LAST PAGE OF
THE BIBLE. IT'S ALL GOING TO
TURN OUT ALL RIGHT."

— Billy Graham

You are the light of the world. . . . Let your light shine
before others, so that they may see your good works
and give glory to Your Father who is in heaven.
— Matthew 5:14-16, ESV

Shine Where You Are

While in a shop in Ireland, a friend was drawn to a beautiful silver cross. It looked as if it had been woven out of straw, with four arms tied at the end and a square in the middle. She learned that it was known as St. Brigid's Cross.

Back in the fifth century, a girl named Brigid went to visit a clan chief on his deathbed. He was incoherent and wildly inconsolable. Brigid probably felt a bit helpless to do much for him, so she settled in at his bedside simply to be there with him.

As she sat, Brigid gathered up a few of the rushes that covered the dirt floor in the room and began weaving a cross. The man watched her, and soon he quieted down enough to start asking questions about what she was doing. He asked what the cross of Christ signified. It is said that Brigid was able to explain the love of Jesus to the man, and he was baptized on his deathbed.

The cross wasn't fancy, and neither is the story. It involves a woman revealing Christ in the simple act of being where God called her and using the resources around her. She literally used what was under her feet to bring Jesus into the room!

We may sometimes feel like our daily work is uninspiring, monotonous, and unimportant to the Kingdom. We are "only" in the office, shuttling kids between activities, or taking an aging parent to doctor's appointments. It sure doesn't feel like we're on the mission field. God's purpose in our lives seems like a goal in the very distant future, but certainly not right now. And that feeling can be so discouraging!

Yet that weariness goes away as we truly grasp this amazing, awesome, eternal truth: no matter the activity—big or small, fascinating or boring—God uses us where we are. We can be a testament to his goodness everywhere if we will only open our eyes and hearts to what He would have us do in each moment. Whether we are in the office with a frustrating coworker who needs a little kindness, with our kids in the car, or at the doctor's office for our parent's appointments, we can shine His light anywhere.

Go about your work today asking God to open your eyes to this truth, and to use you exactly where you are.

Reflect

How might you shine God's light in the little
things of life, exactly where you will be today?

Notes

_____

_____

_____

_____

_____

_____

_____

_____

"PEACE BEGINS
WITH A SMILE."

— Mother Teresa

I have learned to be content whatever the circumstances. I know what it is to be in need, and I know what it is to have plenty. I have learned the secret of being content in any and every situation.
— *Philippians 4:11-12, NIV*

Choose Your Lens

Not long ago, I tried on a pair of jeans at a consignment store that didn't look so great in the shadowy dressing-room mirror. I was taking them back to the rack when I saw a newer mirror in the main room outside, and decided to take a quick second look. Score! The jeans looked completely different once I looked in a better mirror. The mirrors in the dressing room were older and darker, giving a distorted reflection that almost fooled me.

We've all looked at ourselves in distorted mirrors. What we may not realize, though, is that we often see everyday life—especially our challenging circumstances—through a similarly distorted lens. Oh, if only such-and-such was different, I'd feel better, is a common refrain. If only my husband realized what I have to deal with every day is another. The view through that lens makes us discontented and tempts us to grumble.

We try to change our discontentment by changing what we think has led to it. We try to amass more money to get out of that tiny apartment. We try to change how our kids appear to the outside world. We try to force our spouse to do things our way ("The right way!").

The result? Exhaustion. Leading right back to disappointment and discontent.

Or perhaps instead we just grumble a bit about the inconvenience or injustice of the situation. Once those emotions start taking root in our hearts, they often leak out onto our classmates, kids, spouse, coworkers, or friends.

The result? Yet again, exhaustion. Further discontent.

No matter what is going on, we can set aside our "right" to be discontented. Instead, we can take God's challenge to find contentment in every situation. Instead of looking through the lens that shows the most unflattering perspective, let's choose the one that changes everything.

That lens is called gratitude. Gratitude for everything God has allowed us to have that is good (that we might not be focusing on right now) and gratitude that He is sufficient. Not just sufficient to get us through what is difficult—and bear up both us and the scowl on our face—but sufficient to bring us through difficult times with a joyful heart!

Try practicing gratitude today. The facts of the situation won't change, but your perspective on them will. You may not be able to control your circumstances, but every day you do have control over how you view them.

Reflect

Every season of life has its challenges. What can you be
grateful for in the challenge that you are going through right
now? How can you maintain that perspective over time?

Notes

_____

_____

_____

_____

_____

_____

_____

Shift Your Perspective

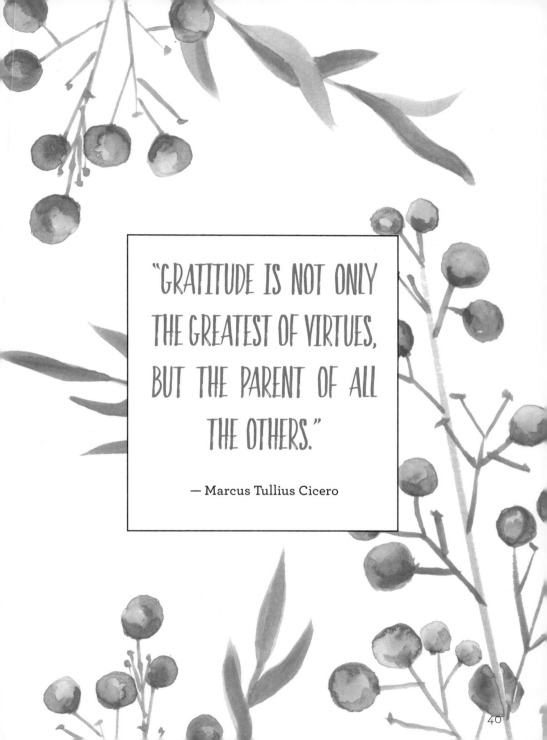

"GRATITUDE IS NOT ONLY THE GREATEST OF VIRTUES, BUT THE PARENT OF ALL THE OTHERS."

— Marcus Tullius Cicero

Blessed are the poor in spirit, for theirs is the kingdom of heaven.
— *Matthew 5:3, NIV*

Seeing Your Need for Him

My teenage daughter had been having a horrible, no good, very bad day. A bad month, really. Her best friends had fractured apart due to personality conflicts, and her closest friend had walked away from her entirely. My naturally shy daughter had finally found a place where she belonged—and now it was all gone.

I gave her lots of hugs and tried to draw her out. My heart hurt as I watched her pain; I longed to be there for her as a support. But day by day I saw her withdraw into herself. "No, I can't explain what's going on. I don't want to talk about it, Mom."

Maybe you know the feeling. Perhaps you are laboring under a load of sadness from a broken relationship, deep hurt, or other betrayal. Maybe you invested your time or energy into something only to have it all taken away. Maybe except for deep feelings of rejection, you are empty.

Take heart, because you are not alone. Someone is hurting right alongside you as He watches your pain. He is longing to hug you and make it better. He wants to be there for you as a support. He wants you to come to Him just as you are, before you have anything figured out. He loves you when you are broken, empty, with nothing to give.

Poor in spirit.

A month into my daughter's ordeal, I went in and prayed for her as usual before bedtime. Finally, after a few moments of inner struggle, she began to truly share, to trust me with her broken heart. And as we walked together before the throne of grace, she began to cast her cares on her heavenly Father and trust that He would heal.

When we set aside our pride, self-consciousness, and self-protectiveness to come before God in our deep need, it is as if we step into a parallel reality. We get a glimpse of the true reality all around us—the eternal reality called the Kingdom of Heaven—and realize that the One who wants to enfold us in His loving arms is also the One sitting on the throne. The sense of fulfillment is so profound that millions look in all the wrong places for it. Yet it is as close as admitting our need for and receiving the love of the One who will make all things new.

Reflect

Where you have brokenness, sadness, or emptiness, are you holding back, or are you coming as you are before God's throne? How will it bless you to come before Him?

Notes

_____

_____

_____

_____

_____

_____

_____

_____

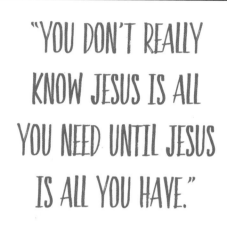

"YOU DON'T REALLY KNOW JESUS IS ALL YOU NEED UNTIL JESUS IS ALL YOU HAVE."

– Tim Keller
Walking With God Through Pain and Suffering.

For he has rescued us from the kingdom of darkness
and transferred us into the Kingdom of his dear Son.
— Colossians 1:13

Underground Espionage Agents

There is a mental shift that will change everything about how we view our lives. We need to realize who we really are. I don't just mean embracing our identity in Christ or the fact that we are daughters of the King. I mean recognizing something much bigger: We are key players in a great war between the Kingdom of God and the kingdom of darkness, and this earth is the primary battlefield.

The anxieties that take our time, create stress, and divert our attention fade into insignificance once we have that perspective. Other things become far, far more important. And suddenly we realize we have a calling beyond ourselves.

The Bible says Satan is "god of this world," (2 Corinthians 4:4), "the commander of the powers in the unseen world" (Ephesians 2:2) and "the ruler of this world" (John 12:31). That doesn't mean that Satan is in ultimate control—our God still reigns over everything—but it does mean that we are living in occupied territory. Once humanity chose sin, the evil one was given the power to rule over this broken world, tempt its people, and spread misunderstanding, division, natural and physical disasters, and spiritual destruction.

And yet, Jesus says that there is another Kingdom! (John 18:36). Once we commit our lives to Christ, we cease being citizens of earth and become citizens of heaven. From that point on, we are called to actively undermine the kingdom in which we are living, on behalf of another King. In other words, we are underground espionage agents. Like the French Underground in World War II, we are called to rescue the captives bound for destruction, to be agents of light in a kingdom of darkness.

Our primary job on this earth is not any of the many hats we wear (wife, girlfriend, mom, grandma, saleswoman, neighbor . . .). Our primary job is to be an agent of Almighty God; to care for people in need; to show kindness when all others would be provoked; to share the Good News through our words and lives; to love one another in a world marked by the evil one's division.

Once we live from this eternal perspective, suddenly we will know which worries, time-wasting distractions, and irritations simply don't matter. We will realize that no matter how much God loves us, this life is not about us. He is calling us to be part of a much bigger story.

Reflect

In which areas have you been distracted by worries and stress in recent days and weeks? How do those worries change if you adopt an eternal perspective? In what one or two areas is God calling you to make an eternal difference for His Kingdom?

Notes

_____

_____

_____

_____

_____

_____

_____

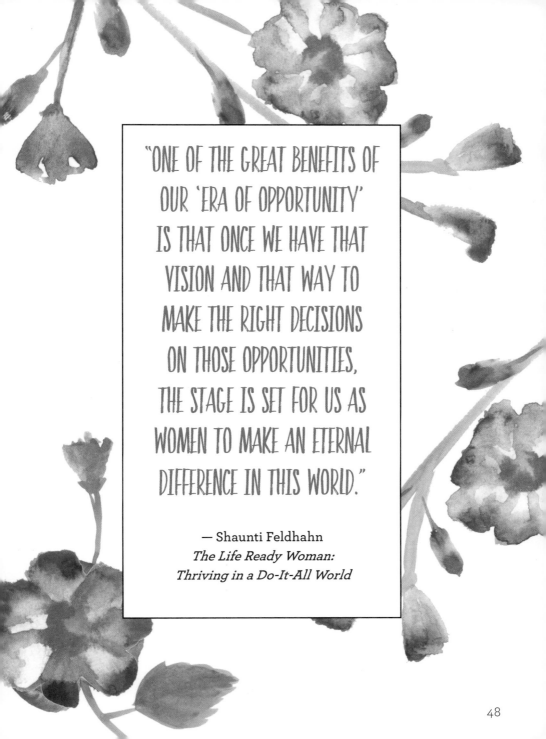

"ONE OF THE GREAT BENEFITS OF OUR 'ERA OF OPPORTUNITY' IS THAT ONCE WE HAVE THAT VISION AND THAT WAY TO MAKE THE RIGHT DECISIONS ON THOSE OPPORTUNITIES, THE STAGE IS SET FOR US AS WOMEN TO MAKE AN ETERNAL DIFFERENCE IN THIS WORLD."

— Shaunti Feldhahn
The Life Ready Woman:
Thriving in a Do-It-All World

This is the day which the Lord has made;
Let us rejoice and be glad in it.
— Psalm 118:24, NASB

Savor Each Day

Every fan of science fiction knows that at warp speed, everything flows by in a blur. And just like any starship worth mentioning, we busy women often rush from point A to point B, from task to task, without taking in the journey in between.

God tells us that one antidote to feeling pressed in on every side is to stop and notice each day and what He is doing with it. After all, we can't "be glad" for God's great works unless we purposefully take in the day that is flowing by.

This reminds me of a great regret of mine that turned into a great lesson. After months of planning our wedding, the actual ceremony seemed to pass in a delightful blur. A few weeks later, my husband mentioned seeing a particular couple who had been at the ceremony but had to miss the reception. I said, "Really? I don't remember seeing them. It all seemed to go so fast—I don't remember much about the ceremony itself."

Jeff smiled sideways. "I remember everything." He then told me that one of his groomsmen, a man who was already married, had taken him aside ahead of time and told him the day could either rush by or be soaked in. "He encouraged me to purposefully enter into it and remember it all. So I made sure to really enjoy every moment."

Shift Your Perspective

I was glad for him, but regretful for me. In some ways, I had missed my own wedding.

Years later, when our kids were born, I heard echoes of that advice from older moms who said, "Oh, enjoy this time. It goes so quickly." This time, I decided, I would not let the warp speed of life turn these precious years into a blur. I have tried to savor and soak in every moment, every stage.

It has been so rewarding. Unlike my wedding ceremony, I have thousands of rich, delightful memories with my kids that will still be precious long after they leave home.

Whether it is about time with family, friends, career, or the use of a particular gift, letting the days slip by and wondering "where did the time go?" is a surefire way to end up with weariness and regret. Let's instead resolve to notice each day, and be glad in it.

Reflect

Are you rejoicing and savoring each day, or is your life one big blur? How can you focus on each moment?

Notes

_____

_____

_____

_____

_____

_____

_____

_____

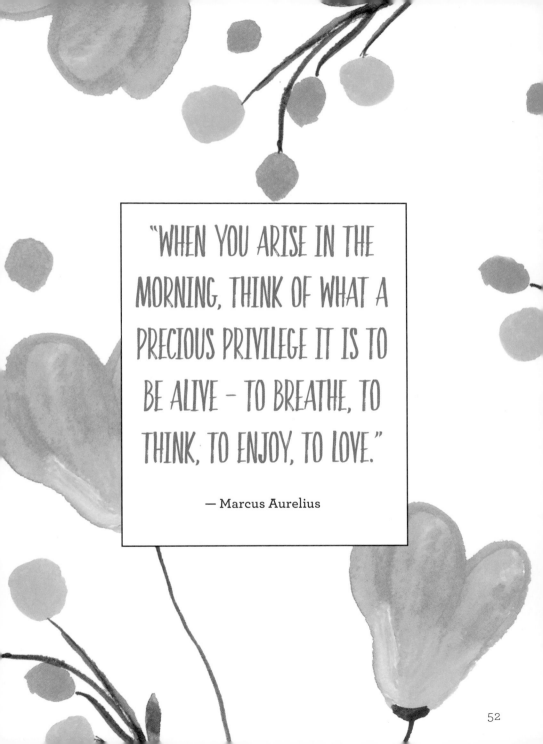

"WHEN YOU ARISE IN THE MORNING, THINK OF WHAT A PRECIOUS PRIVILEGE IT IS TO BE ALIVE – TO BREATHE, TO THINK, TO ENJOY, TO LOVE."

— Marcus Aurelius

*Be honest in your evaluation of yourselves, measuring yourselves
by the faith God has given us. Just as our bodies have many parts
and each part has a special function, so it is with Christ's body.
We are many parts of one body, and we all belong to each other.*
— Romans 12:3-5

The Right Yoke:
Embracing Who You Are NOT

We're often told to be who we are. This also means cheerfully
embracing who we are *not*. Much of our weariness stems from
continuously trying to force a square peg into a round hole.

For several years, that was me. I am a social researcher, and I speak at
a lot of women's retreats, conferences, and marriage seminars. I love
seeing the light bulb go on and watching relationship transformation.
But for a while I dreaded these events because of the many hurting
men and women who came afterward for serious counsel. They would
share heart-wrenching stories of a spouse's betrayal or a child's
addiction and ask for specific advice.

I felt like I should be able to help with their individual hurts and
trials—I mean, what kind of a relationship author was I otherwise?—so
I would listen, try to give advice, and share things from my research
that applied. But I arrived home totally wiped out.

Finally, I realized: I'm not a counselor. I'm a teacher, encourager,
researcher, eye-opener . . . but not a therapist. So instead of feeling like

there was something wrong with me as a relationship author, I started to tell the event organizers, "I'm not a counselor; is there someone I can refer difficult situations to?" And the weight miraculously lifted. I began to listen to the hurting person without pressure, cry with them, pray for them—and refer them to a real counselor.

How has God *not* wired you? Embrace it. Are you an introvert who feels that you "should" like the dinner parties your husband loves to throw? If you two keep fighting over this, embrace the fact that God has wired you to not be an extrovert and that you need recharging with a one-on-one conversation or a good book.

Yes, we need to push ourselves out of our comfort zones to fulfill callings that God asks of us, like hospitality to others and service to our spouse. But God also asks us to see ourselves with sober judgment. So perhaps you can compromise with your husband on the number of get-togethers a month or explain that the day after game night you need downtime. Perhaps you can learn to focus on one-on-one conversation with the friend next to you at the dinner table instead of entering into the buzz of ten other people.

Celebrating who we are—and are not—is the key to fitting joyfully into our place in the body of Christ.

Reflect

Is there something you've been trying to do or be that is not who you are? If it is important for your marriage or life in some way, how can you both embrace who you are not and achieve the necessary goals?

Notes

_____

_____

_____

_____

_____

_____

_____

_____

"IT'S AT THE HEART OF EVERYTHING WE STRUGGLE WITH IN LIFE: LONGING TO BE VALUABLE, TO BE ACCEPTED, TO BE PRIZED, TO BE WORTH SOMETHING TO SOMEBODY, TO HAVE A LIFE THAT MATTERS, AND GOD'S SAYING 'YOU MATTER! I DIDN'T MAKE ANYONE ELSE LIKE YOU. YOU'RE NOT A REPRINT OR A LITHOGRAPH. YOU'RE A ONE-OF-A-KIND, ORIGINAL CREATION OF GOD.'"

— Louie Giglio

Moses' arms soon became so tired he could no longer
hold them up. So Aaron and Hur found a stone for him
to sit on. Then they stood on each side of Moses, holding
up his hands. So his hands held steady until sunset.
— Exodus 17:12

Let Someone Hold Up Your Arms

It gets me every time—my eyes well up as I watch the video of Olympic sprinter Derek Redmond, who massively injured his hamstring midway through his race in the 1992 Barcelona games. He started hopping toward the finish line, his pain palpable as he boldly tried to finish the race, even though he had no hope of winning a medal. Even more touching is what Redmond's father did next. Jim Redmond leapt out of the stands and shook off security guards as he ran to help his son reach his goal. The picture of a father holding up his son as he wept in pain and disappointment makes it one of the most inspiring moments in Olympic history. It's such a clear visual of the raw, messy, beautiful lengths to which we go to serve and love someone we care about.

We like to identify with the father in that story because we can probably imagine doing something similar for someone we love. But if we're honest, there are times in our busy, stressful lives when we are more like the injured runner. It sometimes seems as if we cannot take one more step forward without falling on our face. Whether it's a troubled relationship, a bad diagnosis, our child's behavioral issues at school, job insecurity . . . it all weighs heavy on us, and sometimes it feels like we can't go on.

Create Life-Giving Relationships

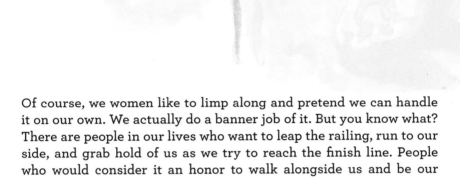

Of course, we women like to limp along and pretend we can handle it on our own. We actually do a banner job of it. But you know what? There are people in our lives who want to leap the railing, run to our side, and grab hold of us as we try to reach the finish line. People who would consider it an honor to walk alongside us and be our companions during the difficult parts of our race.

We need to let them grab our arms and help.

Yes, it means being vulnerable. It means the secret will be out that we cannot handle everything on our own. It feels risky, even embarrassing, to ask for help. But the beauty of allowing someone to help us as we limp toward the finish line brings tears to the eyes—a display of love (both in the giving and the receiving) that reminds us that we are never, ever alone.

Reflect

Have you ever come alongside someone as they struggled?
Think about how honored you felt to help them. Now think
about someone who has offered to help you. Pray for God's
help to set aside your pride and allow them to take hold
of your arms and help you across the finish line today.

Notes

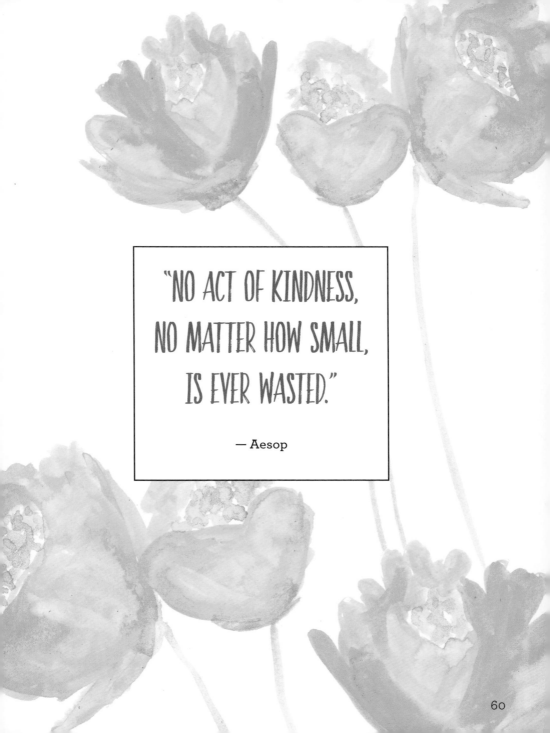

"NO ACT OF KINDNESS,
NO MATTER HOW SMALL,
IS EVER WASTED."

— Aesop

A wife of noble character who can find? She is worth far more than rubies. Her husband has full confidence in her and lacks nothing of value. She brings him good, not harm, all the days of her life.
— *Proverbs 31:10-12, NIV*

The Big, Pretty Picture

When I read about the Proverbs 31 woman, I'm both inspired and overwhelmed by her example. She made food, bought fields, generated profits, bought a vineyard, traded, stayed up late, got up early, clothed her family, stylishly dressed herself, and was a dynamite teacher—all with a whole lot of wisdom. She served the poor, ran her household, was never lazy, and her children adored her. Her husband and community constantly praised her.

Most days I wish I could check just one of those boxes, and I would consider it a big win! It is very easy to feel inferior with this snapshot of womanhood taped to my mirror, calling me to look like this someday.

But the Proverbs 31 woman is not a real woman! This is not Mary or Elizabeth or Rachel. This is not a portrait of an actual woman at some ultimate moment in time when she "has it all together."

Proverbs 31 is a big-picture view of the life of a woman of noble character—not a description of someone who does all these things perfectly, all at once.

This description of a woman of noble character shows us what God

values and gives us something to aspire to. But He also gives us seasons. As newborns grow into toddlers, then adolescents, then young adults, our responsibilities as parents change too. The same applies to our lives as women of faith. There are seasons of young children and there are seasons of empty nesting. There are seasons of community involvement or business, and there are seasons of keeping our heads down and focusing on our family and marriage. There are seasons when we have margin to buy that field and the fixer-upper house on it, and completely different seasons when we can take the time to seek out from afar and cook the perfect paleo/organic/no-red-dye food for our family.

We must not feel bad for devoting ourselves to the season God has called us into.

Are there things we'd like to do once we have more time? Of course! Do we have ministry goals or work aspirations for when the time is right? Absolutely. But let's commit to praying for wisdom to know what God is calling us to do right now to bring Him glory in our particular season. Being obedient to that call will be what paints a beautiful, big picture of a life that points directly to Him.

Reflect

Where do you sense God is calling you to focus in this particular season? What might you be called to set aside, in order to bring Him glory in what you are doing?

Notes

_____

_____

_____

_____

_____

_____

_____

_____

"YOU CAN'T HAVE AN EXCITING, SUCCESSFUL, POWERFUL CAREER AND AT THE SAME TIME WIN THE MOTHER-OF-THE-YEAR AWARD AND BE WIFE AND LOVER EXTRAORDINAIRE. NO ONE CAN. IF YOU SEE SUCCESSFUL, GLAMOROUS WOMEN ON MAGAZINE COVERS PROCLAIMING THEY DO IT ALL, BELIEVE ME, YOU'RE NOT GETTING THE WHOLE STORY."

— Maria Shriver,
Ten Things I Wish I'd Known –
Before I Went Out Into the Real World

Submit yourselves therefore to God. Resist the devil, and he will flee from you. Draw near to God, and he will draw near to you.
— James 4:7-8, ESV

Resist and Draw Near

A friend began to really enjoy her subscriptions to beautiful fashion magazines. Yet she realized it was taking an unexpected toll. She began shopping more, spending far beyond her budget, and became envious of others. Even among women in her Bible study she found herself coveting that necklace, those shoes, that car. It wasn't long before her appetite for the newest clothes and jewelry took a toll beyond the discontent in her heart. Her marriage was in trouble.

Satan knows exactly how to tempt us. And he has come to steal, kill, and destroy. He plots how to pull us away from God. He experiments: which temptation will we follow to our destruction? It may start small—a growing dissatisfaction with our lives as we scroll through social media, compare marital war stories with friends, or look enviously at those who are married while we're still single. Maybe it is the negative chatter in our heads that we are unworthy to be loved, don't deserve that promotion at work, or aren't good at Pinterest-worthy home decorating. Or it could be something big, like debilitating health issues.

Scripture gives a clear two-part solution: immediately resist the devil, and draw near to our heavenly Father. We must stop supporting what the evil one is doing. Maybe it means deleting a social media

app or taping Scripture on your mirror to remind you of God's love for you. Maybe it means committing to resist the sneaky pleasure of complaining about your husband to your girlfriends, and instead saying only positive and loving things to and about him.

Scripture says that if we resist the devil, he will flee. The only way to do that is to draw close to God. He longs for us to have a thriving, close friendship with Him, marked by time in the Bible, prayer, listening, worship, and gratitude for our blessings. When we come near to God, He promises to come near to us.

When my fashion-crazy friend realized what was happening, she knew she had to stop the ugliness growing inside her. She took the hard step of canceling all her fashion magazine subscriptions. She realized she even had to stop looking at those magazines at the gym and the grocery checkout lane. And as she prayed, God immediately helped her notice and be grateful for the many blessings she already had. Which, she realized, was a much more enjoyable way to live.

Reflect

What is one area where the enemy has probably been trying to tempt you to destruction? What one thing can you start doing today to resist him? What can you do that will draw you nearer to God?

Notes

_____

_____

_____

_____

_____

_____

_____

_____

_____

"GOOD JUDGMENT COMES FROM EXPERIENCE. AND A LOT OF THAT COMES FROM BAD JUDGMENT."

— Will Rogers

Let us therefore come boldly to the throne of grace, that we may obtain mercy and find grace to help in time of need.
— Hebrews 4:16, NKJV

Run to the Throne

There is a scene in the movie *Anna and the King* that always chokes me up. A young girl rushes through a massive set of doors into the throne room of a mighty king. Hundreds of supplicants are bowing in reverence (and some in fear) before his throne. Interrupting everything, ignoring every bit of protocol, she rushes past all the people and jumps into the arms of the king. Everyone is shocked . . . but they shouldn't be, because this mighty king is her father. He picks her up, sets aside all the business of the throne room, and carries her out the door to attend to something that is far more important—her.

Sisters, we have a heavenly Father who gives us that same access to Him! He is the King of Kings and the Creator of the universe. He holds the unimaginable depths of the universe together with a word of His power. And yet He tells us we can "come boldly to the throne of grace." What an amazing privilege!

I think we often forget that we are beloved daughters of God. He adores us and longs for us to come to Him and boldly ask Him for help. I remember that feeling as a mom of young toddlers. When my daughter or son fell down at the park and skinned a knee, there was a moment where they would search until they made eye contact with me. And then they would run to me. When that happened, my heart

knew that they trusted me. They knew they were loved. They knew I would kiss them, comfort them, and do whatever I could to help them. I can't help but think that our heavenly Father feels pleased when we do the same with Him.

We so often feel battered and bruised in places that a Band-Aid won't cover. Our hearts feel hurt by relationships that disappoint us. Our minds struggle to keep anxiety at bay. Our bodies feel tired and pulled in a hundred different directions. It requires a certain amount of confidence and vulnerability to trust that if we run boldly to God's throne, He will respond with open arms.

Dare to trust your Father with your heart. You will find grace in your time of need.

Reflect

Close your eyes and imagine yourself running through the doors and into the courts of your heavenly Father. What do you want to approach His throne of grace with today? Write down your prayer, and note anything you think He wants you to trust Him with.

Notes

"FAITH IS TO BELIEVE WHAT
YOU DO NOT SEE; THE REWARD
OF THIS FAITH IS TO SEE
WHAT YOU BELIEVE."

— Saint Augustine

I tell you the truth, the Son can do nothing by himself. He does only what he sees the Father doing. Whatever the Father does, the Son also does.
— *John 5:19*

Do Only What You See Your Father Doing

It had been one of those days. I faced a to-do list mountain, conference calls that went way too long, missed deadlines, and urgent messages from every direction—and I didn't handle it well. After apologizing for the fifth time for snapping at my kids and my husband, I tucked the kids into bed and curled up with a book.

But I quickly sensed that gentle whisper from Holy Spirit, calling me to stop what I was doing and listen. I tried, but my thoughts and worries kept swirling. So I decided to pick just one thing on my to-do list and pray about it; a thorny decision about a particular initiative for my ministry. As soon as my thoughts focused on this worry, the Lord's whisper became so clear: "Is that initiative even what I've called you to focus on right now?"

Honest answer? No, it wasn't. All the things on my to-do list seemed important, but in fact were distracting me from what I knew had to be my two main professional callings for that season: writing my next book and speaking to the groups that had invited me. Worse, they were distracting me from my first calling as a wife and mom.

How can we stop ourselves from ending up with all these "important" things that God hasn't asked us to do? In his landmark study, *Experiencing God*, Henry Blackaby reminds us that rather than picking good things to do and asking God to bless them, we need to look to see where God is working, and go join Him.

Two thousand years ago, Jesus walked around the pool of Bethesda—an area filled with the hurting, sick, and injured. He spoke to and healed just one man. A short time later, He explained why He bypassed the "multitude" at the pool to focus on the one: "I can do nothing by myself. I do only what I see my Father doing. Whatever my Father does, I do." Which also means, by definition, "I do not do those things that my Father isn't doing and leading me to do."

If Jesus was willing to pass up the multitude and trust in His Father's plan, we need to be able to pass up multitudes of opportunities—good things!—in the same way. That will allow us to do the one thing God is doing.

Reflect

What are some seemingly good things in your life that
God may not be doing, and which are getting in the
way of the better things that He has called you to do?

Notes

_____

_____

_____

_____

_____

_____

_____

_____

"WHENEVER YOU SAY YES TO SOMETHING, THERE IS LESS OF YOU FOR SOMETHING ELSE. MAKE SURE YOUR YES IS WORTH THE LESS."

— Lysa TerKeurst,
*The Best Yes: Making Wise Decisions
in the Midst of Endless Demands*

*And this is my prayer: that your love may abound
more and more in knowledge and depth of insight,
so that you may be able to discern what is best and
may be pure and blameless for the day of Christ.*
— Philippians 1:9-10, NIV

It HAS to Be Finished?

Do you ever think you're a bit obsessive about having to finish a particular task you're engrossed in? Most of us have that quirk, and its results cause us a lot of unnecessary regret.

Laurie came to this realization when her kids reached high school. She decided to have a garage sale to sell off all the good-condition grade-school stuff—and have an excuse to trash the stained clothes, smelly roller blades, and partial Playmobil sets.

Soon, though, her goal expanded to include the two walk-in attic storage areas. She describes it this way: "An intoxicating power of minimalism came over me! What a great opportunity to get rid of everything we didn't currently use in case we decided to finish off the largest space into a guest bedroom." Obsessed with getting rid of 25 years of clutter, the simple project mushroomed into a two-headed behemoth.

After several consecutive weeks of preparing for the now-monster garage sale, my friend finally realized that her family was eating only pizzas and McDonald's, and bumming rides to activities. And there may have been a few times that her telephone voice was a tad sweeter to the sales reps than to her family when they interrupted her Great Purge of the Century.

Sound familiar?

My friend asked God for help to break the "It HAS to be FINISHED" cycle. He gave her an idea to help her pay attention to what's really important. She calls it SLOW: **Surrender, Listen, Obey, Walk Away.**

First, I Surrender the "It HAS to be DONE" list to my greater call. Can this activity be done later? Does it really have to be done at all? Listen to that quiet, still Voice inside. If my priorities are wrong, He will tell me. Will I listen? Then Obey. If taking my elderly mother out for coffee is truly the "what is best" thing for now, I need to ask God to help me overcome my compelling drive to finish the task. Then quickly Walk Away from the task before getting sucked back into it. If necessary, I can delegate the task, or perhaps reschedule the completion for another time.

When we are driven by our "It HAS to be done" compulsion, we run over those most in our way—and we often have regrets. By taking it SLOW, we know we gave our best energy and time to the people and projects that truly matter most.

Reflect

When in the past have you been so compelled to finish
something that you ran over a more important priority?
What are you working on now that might need a SLOW approach?

Notes

_____

_____

_____

_____

_____

_____

_____

_____

"WISELY, AND SLOW. THEY STUMBLE THAT RUN FAST."

— William Shakespeare

There remains, then, a Sabbath-rest for the people of God; for anyone who enters God's rest also rests from their works, just as God did from his. Let us, therefore, make every effort to enter that rest.
— Hebrews 4:9-11, NIV

One Day a Week

Talk of "the Sabbath" may take you back to stories of Puritans who sat quietly all Sunday with no noise of any kind. Or maybe you fondly remember Sundays from your childhood, when your extended family went to grandma's after church for fried chicken and visiting. It was a day set apart.

This is not our twenty-first century image of Sabbath. Actually, I'm not sure we have an image of Sabbath at all. Of all the commandments (and this is one of the Ten!), this is the one we most easily ignore. Ironically, it is also the one we most need to balance our busy lives.

I know what you're thinking: there is just too much to do, and you simply can't take a whole day of downtime. I said that many times myself, until I realized that's just pride and lack of trust—the feeling that everything will fall apart or not get done if I'm not working. Let's get over ourselves! If God himself rested (Genesis 2:2), why can't we?

Medical science echoes God's command. "Sabbath" simply means to cease from labor and daily activities. When we are constantly active, our body releases hormones and other chemicals to address the stress. But too much of these chemicals creates issues such as depression, diabetes, anxiety, and more.

Connect with God

Now, a "Sabbath rest" doesn't mean we can't do anything that day. The whole point is renewal, and staring quietly at the walls could be pretty draining! But it does mean God wants us to cease work and trust Him that everything will get done.

A few years back, I was convicted about breaking this commandment. For six years, I wrote syndicated newspaper columns that were due first thing Monday morning. Many Sundays, I spent a few hours holed up with my computer. Then God challenged me to keep the Sabbath, which would mean finishing the column on Saturday or earlier. That seemed impossible, especially since I'm usually out speaking each Saturday.

But I resolved to do it, and it was amazing to watch God work. A column that would normally have taken me five hours to write, would take only two hours—the length of the plane ride back from my speaking engagement. Or a meeting would be cancelled at the last minute, giving me unexpected time to work. It is amazing to see what God does when we resolve in faith to do what He asks.

Reflect

Have you been ignoring God's command for Sabbath rest?
What are the main reasons why? How might you better
honor the Sabbath Day, and keep it holy?

Notes

_____

_____

_____

_____

_____

_____

_____

_____

"TAKE REST; A FIELD
THAT HAS RESTED GIVES
A BEAUTIFUL CROP."

— Ovid

Day 22

Abandon your foolish ways so that you may live,
and proceed in the way of understanding.
— Proverbs 9:6, NET

What Do You See?

Have you seen those pictures that look like two different things depending on your focus? A famous one shows either a very old woman with a scarf pulled over her head, or the profile of a debutante in a fur coat and fancy hat. When you focus on the old lady, she seems haggard, downcast, and forlorn. When you focus on the young debutante, you see a fresh face with a beautiful life ahead. This "Young Girl/Old Woman" illusion was submitted to a humor magazine by British cartoonist William Ely Hill, with the caption, "My wife or my mother-in-law. They are both in this picture—Find them!"

When I first saw the picture, my eye captured the downcast old woman and had to work to see the debutante. And then once I practiced seeing the debutante, I had to make an effort to see the old woman instead. This is how we go through life. Both pictures are there—the beautiful and the ugly, the high and the forlorn. What we focus on determines what we see more of.

God knows this about us, and he knows that a perspective shift from knee-jerk negativity to a default "way of understanding" is essential for a thriving life. When we easily notice our own faults, what someone else did wrong, how someone disappointed us, and so on, we exhaust our ability to see the blessings around us.

Shift Your Perspective

Especially since those "faults" are often optical illusions. That colleague who always submits messy work, at the last minute, may be trying to care for her terminally-ill mother while juggling childcare as a single mom. Wouldn't it make a difference to know that and figure out how to bless instead of curse her? Or when your husband comes home late from work, you can remind yourself that he probably wants to be home for dinner, but that long hours might seem necessary to a husband who is feeling insecure at work and unsure of his ability to provide.

We may not always agree with people, but we can choose to understand. And there's something else: Asking your coworker how things are going at home when she turns in that messy report or thanking your husband for his hard work when he is late (again) is not just a perspective shift: it's grace, just like the understanding and grace that Christ so willingly shows to us.

Reflect

In what areas of life, or with what specific people, do you most
need a perspective shift? How can you look for the good instead?
Is there someone who needs some grace from you today?

Notes

_____

_____

_____

_____

_____

_____

_____

_____

"OUR CULTURE IS ALL ABOUT
SHALLOW RELATIONSHIPS.
BUT THAT DOESN'T MEAN WE
SHOULD STOP LOOKING EACH
OTHER IN THE EYE AND HAVING
DEEP CONVERSATIONS."

— Francis Chan

All praise to God, the Father of our Lord Jesus Christ. God is our merciful Father and the source of all comfort. He comforts us in all our troubles so that we can comfort others. When they are troubled, we will be able to give them the same comfort God has given us.
— 2 Corinthians 1:3-4

Take a Risk

What struggle is most sapping your strength right now? Is it an illness? A heartbreak? A shaky season at work?

A friend of mine, Hannah, is walking a difficult journey with her young adopted son. Put into foster care at the age of four, this little boy has experienced trauma that would bring tears to your eyes. And while adopting him has been an incredible blessing to Hannah, it has also been very hard. As she tries to help her son heal, he often dishes out his worst behavior on her because she is the person he feels safest with.

Hannah's life is exhausting in a way that few understand unless they've lived it themselves. It is lonely. The same is true of your struggles, and mine. God often has people designated to walk with us, but how can we find them? We have to be willing to open up and take the risk of reaching out to those whom God might have put in our lives.

A year or so after Hannah adopted her son, she was discouraged and praying for answers. She met another adoptive mom at the park who seemed nice, and they struck up a conversation. They traded a few

stories, not sharing much. Then my friend tentatively opened up with a very real, raw question. "The therapy. So much therapy, right?" She hoped that this rope she was throwing would be caught, gripped tightly, and pulled to shore by a woman who might know just what type of life she was living.

Hannah's rope was caught. The woman turned to her in excitement that someone else might get her life! From that point on a best-friendship was born that has become a lifeline for both of them. They've been able to bounce ideas off each other, share strategies, and pray for each other. They've been able to comfort each other as they walk similar paths and encourage each other to keep going. They do life together. And it all started with that brave, vulnerable moment.

You never know when your biggest challenge in life could be a common thread that cements a friendship you both need desperately. No matter your situation, be willing to put yourself out there and pray that God will provide people you can love and encourage—and likewise, who can love and encourage you back.

Reflect

In your area of struggle, do you have someone
who can walk alongside you, and you, them?
How might God help you find that person?

Notes

_____

_____

_____

_____

_____

_____

_____

_____

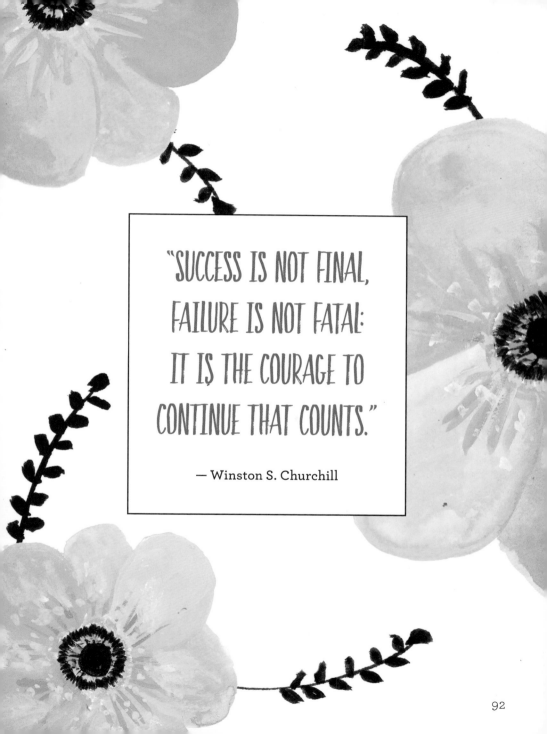

"SUCCESS IS NOT FINAL,
FAILURE IS NOT FATAL:
IT IS THE COURAGE TO
CONTINUE THAT COUNTS."

— Winston S. Churchill

Day 24

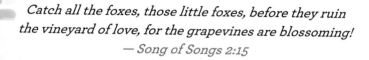

*Catch all the foxes, those little foxes, before they ruin
the vineyard of love, for the grapevines are blossoming!*
— *Song of Songs 2:15*

Don't Let This Fox
Ruin the Vineyard

The Song of Songs is a love song, but is also a metaphor of Christ's love for us. And in this song, Solomon (and Jesus) cry out for the little foxes to be caught before they hurt us or the relationship. The fences protecting the vineyard will easily keep out larger threats, but without vigilance little foxes can creep through small breaches.

One of my friends, the young mother of three small children, often found herself easily overwhelmed and short-tempered. She would go through periods of self-pity, despair, and anger. She was sure she had the most ill-behaved children and the least helpful husband of all time.

God began to speak to her heart. The problem wasn't her children or her husband, the problem was with her. She had one little ongoing habit, one little fox that had been stealing her joy. She would have recognized a larger sin, but this seemingly small sin was creeping in and catching her unaware.

My friend had given in to the temptation to consistently sleep in and skip her morning prayer time. She knew God would understand

Walk in Obedience

that moms are tired! At first, it was just once in a while. But then it multiplied until she had fallen out of the habit of being in God's presence. Without filling her spiritual tank, she was running on empty. And that small fox of a missed devotional time or two had let in a host of his friends. It became easier to meditate on thoughts of anger and despair. It was easier to share in that tidbit of gossip and envy her friend's "perfectly" behaved children.

Those seemingly insignificant little fox sins were taking over and robbing her of the joy and energy that God had reserved just for her. She knew she had to seal the breach, and that prayer and time in God's Word was the only way to strengthen and reinforce her spiritual "fences."

Friends, we need to evaluate: are we stressed, anxious, and irritable mostly because we've let in this fox and his friends? Once we begin making our relationship with God a priority, we will be able to snatch these little foxes as soon as the thought, attitude, or action tries to sneak in. That will do more than anything else to restore our joy.

Reflect

Is the "little fox" of not spending enough time with God robbing you of your joy? How can you repair your spiritual fence?

Notes

_____

_____

_____

_____

_____

_____

_____

"GOD IS ALWAYS SEEKING YOU. EVERY SUNSET. EVERY CLEAR BLUE SKY. EACH OCEAN WAVE. THE STARRY HOSTS OF NIGHT. HE BLANKETS EACH NEW DAY WITH THE INVITATION, 'I AM HERE.'"

— Louie Giglio

Abraham believed God, and it was credited to him
as righteousness, and he was called God's friend.
— James 2:23, NIV

God Calls Me Friend

I was really worried about a big decision that would affect the next few years of my life. I had eagerly wanted to go a particular direction. Now, the more I prayed, the more I felt uneasy about it. One Sunday, my pastor advised that if the disquiet was from God, I needed to trust His leading and turn away from my long-planned path. Yet I still struggled.

The next morning, I felt God asked me a question: "What if it was Cassie telling you to change course? Would you listen if Cassie took your hand, looked into your eyes, and said, 'I can't explain why right now, but trust me: you can't go that way'?" Cassie was one of my dear friends, and I thought, *Of course I would trust her, because she's my friend.*

And then I got it.

We all know about Abraham's strong faith and trust in God. What we sometimes forget is that Abraham and God were friends. And because they were friends, Abraham was willing to trust God enough to do whatever He asked—even walking up that mountain to sacrifice Isaac (Genesis 22:1-19). He showed that God could count on him, and he knew he could count on God. Friends count on each other.

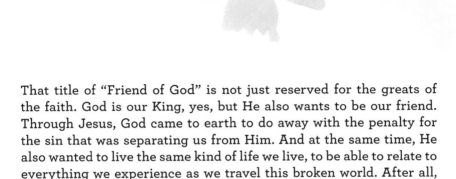

That title of "Friend of God" is not just reserved for the greats of the faith. God is our King, yes, but He also wants to be our friend. Through Jesus, God came to earth to do away with the penalty for the sin that was separating us from Him. And at the same time, He also wanted to live the same kind of life we live, to be able to relate to everything we experience as we travel this broken world. After all, shared experiences bond friends together.

Is there something you need to decide today? Something you're worrying about? Perhaps you have to decide how to pay the bills, whether or not to rescue your adult daughter from her poor choices, and how to cope with the pain of your divorce. Listen to the reassurance from the One who is (or wants to be) your best friend. Whatever course He is leading you to, He asks you to trust Him. Choose to trust God as your best friend, the One who will always do what is best for you. He is the friend who will never let you down.

Reflect

In what areas are you struggling with worry?
How does thinking of God as your perfect best
friend change how you view those situations?

Notes

_____

_____

_____

_____

_____

_____

_____

_____

"WHEN GOD PUSHES YOU TO THE EDGE OF DIFFICULTY, TRUST HIM FULLY BECAUSE TWO THINGS CAN HAPPEN. EITHER HE'LL CATCH YOU WHEN YOU FALL OR HE WILL TEACH YOU HOW TO FLY."

— Author Unknown

The man answered, "'You must love the Lord your God
with all your heart, all your soul, all your strength, and
all your mind.' And, 'Love your neighbor as yourself.'"
"Right!" Jesus told him. "Do this and you will live!"
— *Luke 10:27-28*

Idols, Idols, Everywhere

When Jeff and I lived in New York City, our pastor was the well-known apologist Tim Keller. He rarely used props onstage, so my attention was captured one Sunday when he casually leaned on a barista-style table as he taught. Tim's sermon that day was on idolatry, and he rested his weight against the table for a long time.

We don't tend to view "idols" these days as a current issue—they seem like a problem from thousands of years ago, when people sacrificed bulls at the feet of shiny statues. There are no shiny statues in my home, and I'm guessing there are none in yours. But we do have idols today—and it is one of the main reasons for the stress and worry in our lives.

Idols are anything we rely on—lean on for support—other than God. Those things will never support us well, and that is why idolatry is a recipe for anxiety and pain.

As Tim illustrated his sermon that day, he said something like this: "If this table breaks, or gets yanked out from under me, I'll fall on the floor. That's how you can know that you've made something an idol: if it were to disappear, you'd feel insecure, worried, bereft, or even unable to function."

Ladies, it is so easy to rely on things other than God, without realizing it. For example, we may not think of ourselves as materialistic, and yet how many of us have made money an idol? I know that I feel a lot more secure when I have a buffer in the bank account, and I feel panicky and insecure when that buffer isn't there. Yet I need to trust in God's ability and goodness to provide, not in the money in my account!

We need to ask ourselves: What is it that would leave me feeling pretty bad if it were to go away? Is it my kid's prowess in sports? Is it my status as a rising star at work? Is my home, appearance, volunteer work, technology, shopping, food, drink, age, money—or my position as friend, girlfriend, or wife—affecting my mood and ultimate feeling of balance?

We have to depend on God with our entire heart, soul, strength, and mind. He's the only one who can hold us up. Nothing earthly (no matter how easy it is to lean on) can do the job.

Reflect

Stop and take an honest assessment of the top three things that you "lean" on—those things that, if they were to suddenly go away, would make you feel bad about yourself, worried, or stressed (work? social media? children's activities? personal appearance?). How can you start putting these things into proper balance, as blessings from God rather than something to be leaned on instead of Him?

Notes

"THERE IS BUT ONE GOOD;
THAT IS GOD. EVERYTHING
ELSE IS GOOD WHEN IT
LOOKS TO HIM AND BAD
WHEN IT TURNS FROM HIM."

— C.S. Lewis,
The Great Divorce

There is a time for everything, and a season
for every activity under the heavens.
— Ecclesiastes 3:1, NIV

Seasons of Life

In the South, the weather is fickle as winter changes to spring. Several days of bitter cold are followed by a week of warm, beautiful weather. Then, snap! Back to cold. With the premature warm weather, jonquils and azaleas begin to bloom. But it's not quite the right time, and they'll die with the next cold snap. I wish I could tell the daffodils in my yard, "Wait! The right season is coming, just wait for it!"

And yet—how often have I not heeded my own advice when it comes to the seasons of life?

As we saw earlier, God has clearly designed life with seasons. Something that will allow us to thrive in one stage may be damaging in another. For example, as single young adults we are available for long hours in work and ministry in a way that can be quite damaging if we try to do that once we are married and have children at home. Yet, if we are eventually called to marriage, those single years are also the season to find our life partner. So it can be just as damaging to spend all our time on long work hours and none on the personal purpose of that season.

It is easy to rebel against "confining" boundaries and not recognize God's wisdom in creating them. For many years, my friend Aimee

was extremely career minded and busy. Then Aimee and her husband adopted two young toddlers and decided she would stay home with them. Since she was an older mom, and her friends' kids were already in school, her friends had plenty of time for volunteering, tennis teams, and other activities. Aimee was invited to it all. "Hey, since you're at home, could you help us with this fundraiser?" "We are going on a girls' weekend to a cabin, want to come?" And she often did—even if it meant hiring a sitter to help.

Before she knew it, Aimee's days were filled with activities but she was feeling overwhelmed, unfulfilled, and underappreciated. Finally Aimee realized that her friends were in a different season of life. Her own children needed her more than the fundraisers, girls' weekends, and other good things she could do. As she switched priorities, she found that her days were just as busy but her heart was full. That's the way it works with seasons. In the right time, we thrive.

Reflect

What season of life are you in? Are you embracing it,
or trying to do things meant for another season?
What might God want you to change?

Notes

_____

_____

_____

_____

_____

_____

_____

_____

"IT'S SO TEMPTING TO TRY TO DO IT ALL, SO AS NOT TO MISS OUT. BUT TO DO ALL OF THOSE 'GOOD THINGS' MEANS YOU'LL DO NONE OF THEM WELL."

— Shaunti Feldhahn,
The Life Ready Woman:
Thriving in a Do-It-All World

Wherever you find jealousy and fighting, there will be trouble and every other kind of wrong doing. But the wisdom that comes from heaven is first of all pure. Then it gives peace. . . . It is full of loving kindness. . . . It has no doubts and does not pretend to be something it is not.
— James 3:16-17, NIV

Cancel Comparisons

We have an odd challenge in today's social media age: feeling blessed where God has us, despite the never-ending cycle of posts by others who document their #blessedmoments, #blessedwife, #blessedmama, #bestfamilyever. Everyone else seems to have the #perfectlife.

Don't get me wrong: there's nothing wrong with being outspoken about feeling blessed! The problem comes when we take our eyes off our own blessings and feel jealous of the #blessings of others.

Wow, what I wouldn't give for her remodeled kitchen. Look at her kids and husband cavorting with their dog at the beach. Wish I could afford to do that for Labor Day.

Somehow whenever we dwell on how beautiful our friend's house looks or how toned her arms are or how deliriously happy she is with her husband, it takes a little air out of our own sails. In our heads, we know that social media posts are never the whole story, but they sure paint a pretty picture. And it seems even more pretty when we look around our 1980's-era kitchen filled with dirty dishes and piles of mail while wearing yoga pants that we may or may not have slept in last night.

How do we navigate this digital age without feeling like we're being fed near-constant reminders of everything we're not? Since moving to a deserted island with a weak wireless signal is not an option, what then?

God says that we need pure, wise, loving kindness toward others instead. We need to be sincerely delighted that our friend finally was able to get her dream kitchen, or that trip to the beach. We also need sincere gratitude for what we have. Both will help us repent of and set aside envy.

God knows what comparison does to our hearts. And you know what? It's a sin. It takes our attention away from the gratitude we should have for our own lives and turns our eyes to what we wish we had. When we feed our minds and hearts with images of someone else's one-dimensional perfect online life, we are missing our own three-dimensional life right before our eyes.

Friends, what we focus on can either steal our joy or build it. And God wants us to live that #blessedlife by being in grateful relationship with Him. Let's stop comparing ourselves to others. Let's keep our #EyesOnJesus. If we're going to emulate anyone's life, let it be His.

Reflect

Where are you most tempted to compare? What plan
can you put in place today to minimize comparison
and spur gratitude instead? Do you need to limit
social media time? Start keeping a gratitude journal?

Notes

_____

_____

_____

_____

_____

_____

_____

_____

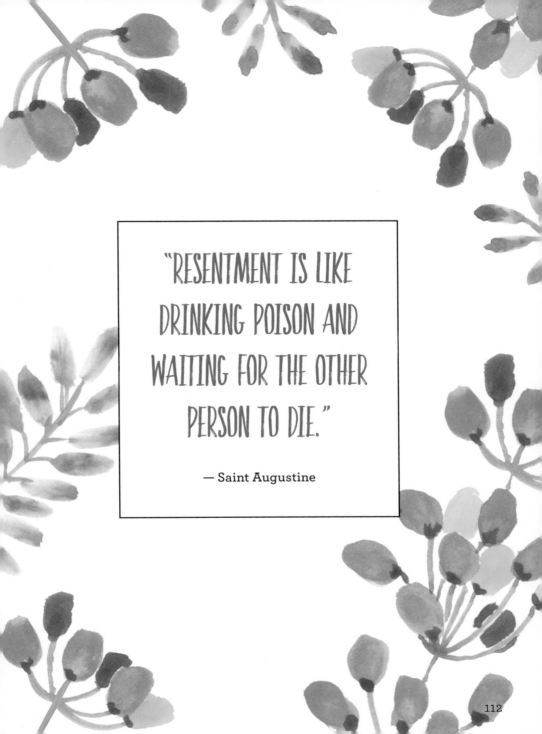

"RESENTMENT IS LIKE
DRINKING POISON AND
WAITING FOR THE OTHER
PERSON TO DIE."

— Saint Augustine

The Lord will fight for you; you need only to be still.
— Exodus 14:14; NIV

Let Him Fight the Battle

I'm wired to be a doer. If there's a problem, I get antsy until I figure out how to fix it. If there's a roadblock, well now, there's got to be a way around it. If the insurance company denies my claim, I file an appeal. When a sales presentation goes awry, I call and apologize, trying to reestablish the relationship right away.

But what happens when we need something to change, and there's nothing we can do?

One woman I know was appalled when she moved offices and discovered that no one on the new team would speak to her. She was treated as invisible. Her coworkers passed her in hallways and sat just feet away, never acknowledging her presence. No acts of friendliness made a dent. She tried repeatedly to talk to her bosses about it, but they refused to listen. Nothing worked.

As my friend relayed her story, I shuddered. The exact same thing happened at my first college waitressing job, when my secretly racist supervisor discovered I had gone to Homecoming with a black friend. She literally never spoke to me again, passing her instructions through others.

Being shunned makes us feel shamed and helpless. My friend described driving home every night, month after month, bewildered

and in tears. In her hopelessness and exhaustion, she even stopped praying.

Then her job ended abruptly, giving her long hours of reflection time. And she realized a few things. First, just as her coworkers ignored her, she had been ignoring God. Just as she longed to connect with her coworkers, her heavenly Father longed to connect with her.

One of the things God wanted to tell her, if she had listened, was to stop flailing around. She was not called to fight this battle. Instead, she was called to stand in trust and watch as God fought the battle and worked out His plan for her life.

Friends, if you are getting beaten up in a certain battle, realize that there are some fights God does not want us to take on. They are His. My friend later realized that God's answer was to remove her from a job she would not quit on her own. God's answer in my situation was for my supervisor to be fired. Both were God's hand at work. Let us resolve to let Him work, and be still.

Reflect

How have you been fighting battles recently that you might not be called to fight on your own? Thinking back, are there instances where you realize God was fighting for you? Write them down as reminders for the future.

Notes

_____

_____

_____

_____

_____

_____

_____

_____

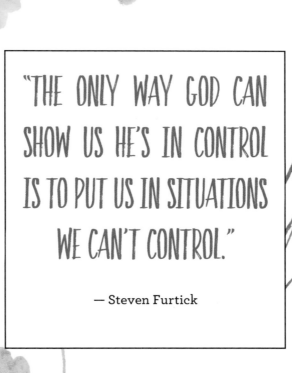

"THE ONLY WAY GOD CAN SHOW US HE'S IN CONTROL IS TO PUT US IN SITUATIONS WE CAN'T CONTROL."

— Steven Furtick

Gracious words are a honeycomb, sweet
to the soul and healing to the bones.
— Proverbs 16:24, NIV

A Little More Honey,
A Lot Less Vinegar

We've all heard the saying, "You can catch more flies with honey than with vinegar," right? We all agree with it! The problem is, vinegar comes out a lot more naturally, especially when we're stressed. As one friend and I discussed the relationship chaos in her life, she said, "Look, I call it like I see it. I know some people don't like it, but that is their problem, not mine." Yet she wants more close people in her life than she has. In other words, it is her problem.

So many of us have a blind spot about what comes out of our mouths. It is as if you set up a sales booth right in the center of town to sell your grandma's favorite sauerkraut dish. You call to anyone who will listen, "it's wonderful!" But every time someone walks near, they wrinkle their noses at the pungent, vinegary smell and quickly cross to the other side of the street.

It is hard to admit that we could be the ones causing our own relationship stress.

Imagine the difference once you get rid of all the sauerkraut and purposefully stock your booth with fresh-baked honey muffins and cakes instead. The smell wafts through the air and people flock to

you. They are drawn to that sweet smell. They want more of what you have to offer.

As you avoid words of vinegar and share pleasant words instead, those around you receive life and health. And they want to be with you, which means they in turn will speak life to you, forgive your foibles, and so on.

We have to not only retrain our brains to focus on what is good and lovely about others, but to *say* what is good and lovely about others. We need to avoid the unnecessary vinegar. That doesn't mean we can't discuss real issues or problems, but it does mean that we try wherever possible to address those problems with kind words, not cruel ones.

Our words can either be sharp vinegar or sweet honey to the people around us. And it all starts with whether we will choose to avoid harsh words and a tone that will drive others away, and instead focus on kind words that draw others in. Because as we say the words to others that are sweet to their soul, it heals us as well.

Reflect

In what situations do words of vinegar tend to
come out of you, perhaps without you even realizing it?
How can you be sure to share sweet words instead?

Notes

_____

_____

_____

_____

_____

_____

_____

_____

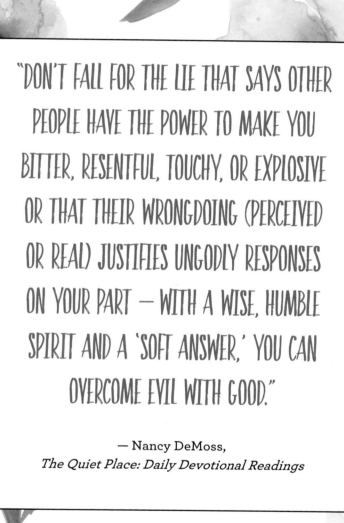

"DON'T FALL FOR THE LIE THAT SAYS OTHER PEOPLE HAVE THE POWER TO MAKE YOU BITTER, RESENTFUL, TOUCHY, OR EXPLOSIVE OR THAT THEIR WRONGDOING (PERCEIVED OR REAL) JUSTIFIES UNGODLY RESPONSES ON YOUR PART — WITH A WISE, HUMBLE SPIRIT AND A 'SOFT ANSWER,' YOU CAN OVERCOME EVIL WITH GOOD."

— Nancy DeMoss,
The Quiet Place: Daily Devotional Readings

The Lord is my shepherd; I shall not want. He makes me lie down in green pastures. He leads me beside still waters. He restores my soul.
— Psalm 23:1-3, ESV

Adrenaline or Oxygen?

When my children were young, they would expend every last ounce of energy before finally collapsing from total exhaustion. I once watched my toddler son fall asleep, face first, in his bowl of mac 'n cheese. Once overtiredness kicked in, my kids could do nothing until their little bodies got rest.

It's kind of cute to watch . . . in preschoolers.

It's not so funny when it's us, is it? Especially because "doing nothing" is often not an option. The lunches need to get packed, the client report finished by Tuesday, the kids' homework reviewed . . . I've never yet done a noodle face-plant, but I've sure felt like I was about to, after pushing myself to the point of utter depletion.

Here's the problem: many of us are literally running on adrenaline instead of a healthy foundation of rest, deep breaths, prayer time, God-directed pacing, and peace. Every day, we use up all our energy to get things done and solve the crisis of the moment. When the next crisis hits ("Wait, you wanted that report finished *today*?"), the only option is a surge of adrenaline to propel us forward.

But God did not design our bodies that way. Adrenaline is His provision

for an emergency fight-or-flight situation, not daily life. When it builds up in our system, we may suffer from anxiety, insomnia, fatigue, or a weakened immune system. We can also become used to drawing on adrenaline to get things done and find it harder and harder to get things done without it. If you've ever procrastinated because you felt like you just couldn't get into the groove on that report (or on creating the 230 party favors you promised for a friend's wedding), then suddenly felt concentration rushing in right before the deadline, you have experienced adrenaline dependence.

Adrenaline, ultimately, is driven by fear. This is not the abundant life God has for us!

If you feel like you have nothing but adrenaline to draw on, ask God to show you what to change. I realized I had to make one major lifestyle switch (declining certain speaking trips, even though it meant less revenue for the ministry) and one habit change (strictly limiting how much news I read, since I used it to procrastinate). In addition, just as you need oxygen to fuel your body, you need deep soul breaths of God's Word. He will restore your soul.

Reflect

Are you running on adrenaline or oxygen? What lifestyle,
health, or habit changes do you need to make so that
you can take in deep breaths and restore your soul?

Notes

_____

_____

_____

_____

_____

_____

_____

_____

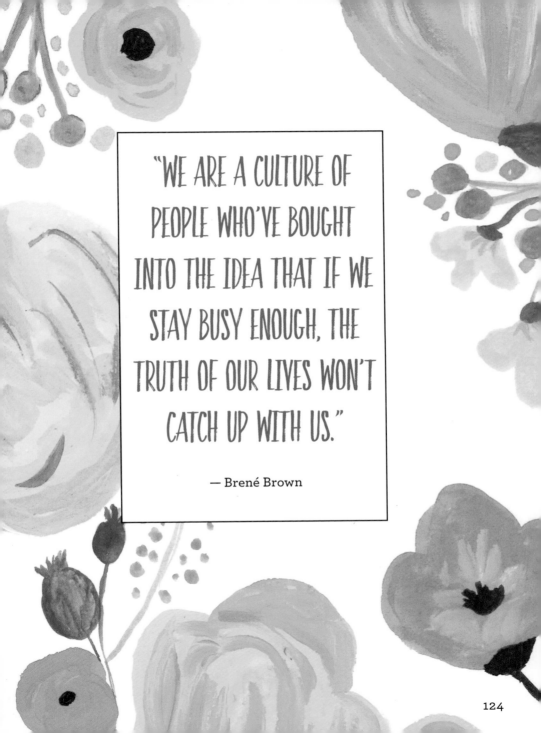

"WE ARE A CULTURE OF PEOPLE WHO'VE BOUGHT INTO THE IDEA THAT IF WE STAY BUSY ENOUGH, THE TRUTH OF OUR LIVES WON'T CATCH UP WITH US."

— Brené Brown

Who are you to judge someone else's servants? They stand or fall before their own Lord (and they will stand, because the Lord has the power to make them stand). . . . So let's strive for the things that bring peace and the things that build each other up.
— *Romans 14:4, 19, CEB*

Either Side of Judgment

Have you ever noticed that while it is all too easy to judge others—or worry about their judgment of us—it is actually a bit exhausting?

A friend of mine was attending a Christmas program at her child's school. As the children lined up to perform, the woman next to her elbowed her and said, "See Susie in the third row? I don't know how she can always come to these programs in those fancy outfits. Everyone knows her family can hardly even put food on the table." My friend felt uncomfortable and didn't quite know what to say, so she just shrugged and kept silent.

Months later, my friend lost her job—and a sizable portion of her family's income with it. That summer, church camp and activities for her children were provided through scholarships and the generosity of others. Her parents gave her funds for a back-to-school shopping trip. But as she was at the mall with her children, carrying sacks and bags full of clothes and shoes from nice shops, the memory of the woman at the Christmas program suddenly rang through her head.

My friend felt ill. She was the only one who knew that her parents had paid for this shopping trip. For the next few hours, she worried she

might run into someone who knew of their difficult financial situation. She certainly couldn't enjoy the simple gift of time with her kids and the blessing that her parents had given her.

We don't know the details about every situation or about how God is working in another person's life. We are not qualified to judge. Yet it is so easy to get caught up in evaluating another person's marriage, child-rearing skills, spending habits, or even their Christian walk. It is just as easy to get caught up in worrying what others think of us.

The Scriptures tell us clearly that we are all accountable to our Master—and only to our Master. The call to be holy includes setting aside our judgment of others and our fear of others. Either a judgmental spirit or a fearful spirit requires energy and creates emotional baggage we were not meant to carry. Let's lay down the exhausting burden of either side of judgment, and take up the call to refresh and encourage others instead.

Reflect

Have you found yourself in "judging mode?"
"Fearful of what others think" mode? In which area
do you need to be more careful to look to God alone?

Notes

_____

_____

_____

_____

_____

_____

_____

_____

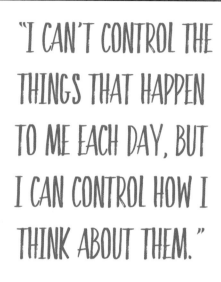

"I CAN'T CONTROL THE
THINGS THAT HAPPEN
TO ME EACH DAY, BUT
I CAN CONTROL HOW I
THINK ABOUT THEM."

— Lysa TerKeurst
Unglued

For though we live in the world, we do not wage war as the world does. The weapons we fight with are not the weapons of the world. On the contrary, they have divine power to demolish strongholds. We demolish arguments and every pretension that sets itself up against the knowledge of God, and we take captive every thought to make it obedient to Christ.
— 2 Corinthians 10:3-5, NIV

Knowing the Real Deal

This world is scary, isn't it? Terrorism, war, financial chaos, human slavery, abandoned kids, injustice, disease . . . it's enough to sink anyone's heart into despair. Or those worries closer to home: the sick child or the struggle with infertility, the huge expenses and unpaid bills.

We need to remind ourselves: It seems hopeless because the enemy of our souls wants us to think it is hopeless. But it's not!

The Bible promises us that we have weapons to fight this war against the darkness. Divine power, in fact. God's power demolishes anything that grabs our hearts with a dark, viselike grip or wages war in our minds to tear us away from trusting in Jesus.

We are invited into this divine power by taking captive all our thoughts and making them obedient to Christ. We do that by knowing Him and His voice, so we can discern His whispers in our thoughts and rebuke the counterfeit whispers from the most talented liar in history. We must be able to hear what our Lord is telling us to think and do about

Have No Fear

those deep concerns (do I look for a new job that pays better, or do I sense that God is asking me to watch for a different solution?), and then walk forward.

In John MacArthur's book, *Reckless Faith*, he describes how Federal agents learn to identify counterfeit money: they don't study the counterfeits, they study genuine bills until they master the look of the real thing. Then when they see the bogus money, they recognize it.

Friends, we need to commit to truly knowing and studying Jesus rather than studying all that is wrong in our world. Just as with any other friend, we get to know Jesus by spending purposeful time with Him. That means digging into the Bible. It means going to church and worshiping and participating in a community of believers. It means praying—and listening—to Him. Knowing Jesus as the real deal will help us focus more on what He is doing and less on the distractions of the enemy.

The old hymn captures it well: "Turn your eyes upon Jesus, look full in His wonderful face. And the things of the earth will grow strangely dim, in the light of His glory and grace."

Reflect

What fear or worry is trying to capture your mind and heart today?
What can you do to take those thoughts captive and focus on Jesus
whenever they arise? Listen to praise music? Spend a few minutes
reading the Bible? Write down that habit, then begin practicing it.

Notes

_____

_____

_____

_____

_____

_____

_____

_____

_____

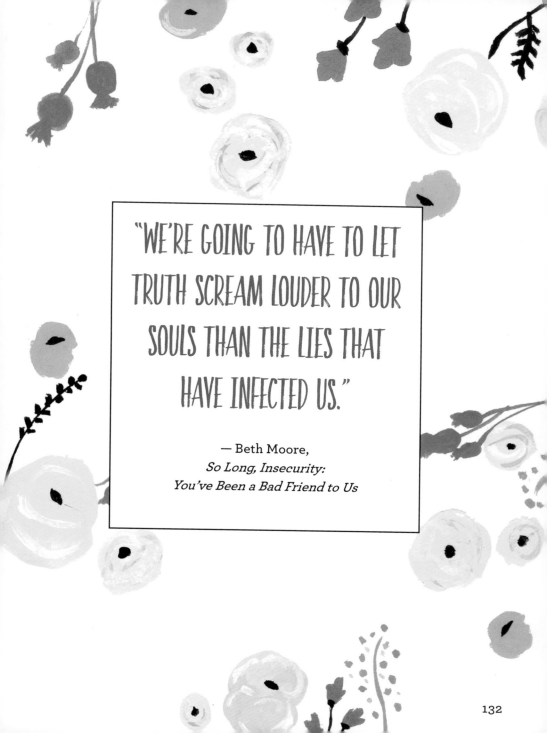

"WE'RE GOING TO HAVE TO LET TRUTH SCREAM LOUDER TO OUR SOULS THAN THE LIES THAT HAVE INFECTED US."

— Beth Moore,
So Long, Insecurity:
You've Been a Bad Friend to Us

Your word is a lamp to my feet and a light to my path.
— *Psalm 119:105, ESV*

Following the Map

It was a rare day off at the guest ranch where I worked during my college summers, a perfect day for a hike. A group of us planned to hit the familiar trail out of the valley where the ranch was nestled. Then one person suggested an adventure: an unknown path to find a cliff that was rumored to have a legendary view. "Sure! Why not?!" Famous last words.

Soon we were out of sight of all known landmarks. The terrain got more steep, more wooded, and more rocky. As we ventured deeper into the unknown, some of us college-age kids were thinking what no one was saying: are we sure we know how to get home?

Within an hour, we found the cliff and the legendary view was duly admired. But for all our efforts to get there, we didn't linger. The afternoon sun was dipping fast, and we headed back down the mountainside, anxious to get back to familiar territory.

That's when I realized: we were truly lost.

Have you ever had that feeling? Maybe you weren't physically lost, but you felt totally lost in unfamiliar territory nonetheless. Maybe you are married and feeling lonely, unsure of your husband's love.

Or maybe your fiancé broke off your engagement. Perhaps you lost your job, or your church is going through a devastating split. You feel totally abandoned by God and want to pull away.

That day in the mountains, we had all those "lost" feelings. Several of us wanted to set out in a particular direction because we were absolutely certain that the ranch was that way—until the most seasoned hiker among us pulled out a compass and a map. He said, "I know you feel like this is the way we should go. But out here, you can't always trust your feelings. Always follow the compass."

Friends, we can't always trust our feelings. But we can trust the compass of God's Word. You may be feeling abandoned or worried, but the Bible clearly says God is always with us, so we do not need to be afraid. We need to trust that those words are 100 percent true—and act like it.

That day in the mountains, our group turned away from the path our feelings would have chosen and followed the compass, and it brought us safely home. You can trust that God's Word will always do the same.

Reflect

Is there an area where your feelings are directing
you in one direction, but God's Word would direct
you in another? What direction will you choose?

Notes

_____

_____

_____

_____

_____

_____

_____

_____

"FAITH IS ACTING LIKE GOD IS TELLING THE TRUTH."

— Priscilla Shirer

But to all who believed him and accepted him,
he gave the right to become children of God.
— *John 1:12*

Whom Do You
See in the Mirror?

As women, we wear many hats: wife, mother, aunt, grandmother, sister, friend, employee. . . . Yet more than any of those titles, the most important is daughter of a heavenly Father. A child of God. Many of us know that with our minds, yet we have great difficulty simply resting in that identity in our hearts. In fact, we do the opposite of rest; we burn the candle at both ends because we feel so much better about ourselves when we accomplish more.

One woman told me that her life had, without her realizing it, become wrapped up in how much she was able to get done. She cared for her family, attended school to further her career, and earned awards and accolades. A full calendar proved she was important.

Then everything stopped. One day she couldn't get out of bed. She'd been ignoring some serious symptoms, and now discovered she had lupus. It had probably lain dormant for years, but the stress she'd been putting on herself triggered a massive flare. Now, her immune system was attacking her own body. She had to put the brakes on her busyness and move into the slow lane.

Eventually she came to see that lupus was a strange gift to her. She

took a long, hard look in the mirror and realized she'd been trying to fill a need with all those accomplishments and accolades—a need only God could fill. She had to truly see that she wasn't special because of anything she had done, but because God had created her to be uniquely her. His child.

Have you been allowing your identity as a child of God to get crowded out by life's demands? Do you feel important because of how much you can accomplish in one day? Do you secretly feel special because your calendar is so full? Sisters, we've been finding our value in things other than our identity in Christ. God loves you for you, because you are His, and it doesn't matter if tomorrow you accomplish one thing or twenty. Nothing will cause Him to love you less or more.

Take a moment and really relax in that knowledge, in the presence of your Father. Hang out with Him. Just as you long to spend time with your family, your heavenly Father longs to spend time with you. God wants you to know how special you are, just because you are His child.

Reflect

When you take a long, hard look in the mirror, do you see a beloved child of God or someone trying to find value and purpose in activities or a full schedule? Today, ask God to help you really grasp your identity as a daughter of the King.

Notes

_____

_____

_____

_____

_____

_____

_____

_____

"WE ARE ACCEPTED
NOT BECAUSE OF WHO
WE ARE, BUT BECAUSE
OF WHO GOD IS."

— Jennifer Rothschild

Do not let me be disgraced, or let my enemies rejoice in
my defeat. No one who trusts in you will ever be disgraced.
— Psalm 25:2-3

Don't Listen to the Rooster

Right before Jesus was arrested and crucified, the disciples met for the Last Supper. Peter adored his rabbi and friend. Can you imagine Peter's dismay when Jesus looked him in the eye and point-blank told him that he would soon betray Him — not once but three times — before the rooster crowed? Peter was indignant, but of course that's what happened. As soon as Jesus was arrested and push came to shove, Peter denied knowing his best friend to save his own skin. Once. Twice. Three times.

Cock-a-doodle-doo. Can you imagine the abject shame that splintered Peter's soul once he realized what he had done?

Shame often sits embedded like a splinter in our souls because we humans tend to love reliving past mistakes. It seems crazy, but we replay foolish decisions and ways we've hurt others—even when we are Christ followers who believe in forgiveness and grace.

It doesn't have to be that way. Peter wept bitterly. But when Jesus was resurrected and met with His disciples, part of His time was spent reconciling with Peter. He offered Peter the opportunity to reengage and reconnect with Him—essentially a chance to change the end of

the story. Isn't it just like Jesus to take our deepest regrets and wipe them clean? But that wasn't really the end of the story, was it? After all, every single morning for the rest of his life, Peter probably woke up to the sound of a rooster's crow. It could have been a daily reminder of his deepest shame. Peter likely had to choose to accept God's grace and forgiveness, and let regret be wiped away rather than replaying his failure and letting it fester.

We have to do the same thing. That friend we hurt so badly, whom we see at church every week. The mistake that got us fired, and the bank balance that condemns us every time we pay monthly bills. God knows all of it, and He wants us to accept His forgiveness for all of it. And that means living in forgiveness, not replaying regret.

The truth is, the rooster will crow. It's just a matter of what we choose to hear. God desires for it not to be a reminder of our shame but to be the sweet, sweet sound of His amazing grace.

Reflect

Is there a past regret or mistake that you replay, that sits like a splinter in your soul? What is your "rooster" that reminds you of it, and how can you reframe it so it reminds you daily of God's grace and forgiveness?

Notes

_____

_____

_____

_____

_____

_____

_____

_____

"GRACE MEANS THAT ALL OF YOUR MISTAKES NOW SERVE A PURPOSE INSTEAD OF SERVING SHAME."

— Mike Foster

Commit to the Lord whatever you do,
and he will establish your plans.
— Proverbs 16:3, NIV

Know When to Pull Yourself Off the Field

I was training an elite group of up-and-coming female leaders at a huge corporation. As part of our role-playing case study, they worked on a fictional workplace scenario: after some financial setbacks, their unit had a big opportunity that might keep their whole department afloat. It would require "all hands on deck," overtime, and weekends for the next six months. Then each person was told they now had a unique personal crisis to juggle (such as a husband diagnosed with cancer, a young child needing speech therapy at 4 p.m. three days a week, or elderly parents who needed help finding and moving into assisted living).

The women crafted a solution for their particular conundrum, then did a role-play to present it to a senior male executive.

The team with the cancer case was first up, with a carefully-crafted solution that involved working early hours and late nights to make up for missing time for the husband's chemo, and enlisting others to cover for them while they were gone. The women leaders were completely confounded by the executive's response: "Your proposal is heroic and admirable, but completely unrealistic. I didn't believe a word of it."

Awkward silence.

Every competent woman knows that you do whatever it takes to get the job done well. But just as important, we need to recognize when circumstances render us unable to get our job done well. Just as a good soccer player would never insist on playing on a badly sprained ankle, thereby putting the whole team at risk, we sometimes need to realize when we're actually doing our team—and ourselves—a disservice if we do not pull ourselves off the field for a time. As the tough executive put it that day, "Yeah, we might need you—but your husband needs you more."

How many times do we realize we have overcommitted or encountered unforeseen circumstances that leave us incapable of finishing our obligations? We need to learn when to pull ourselves off the field for a time, wave our white flag of humility, and enjoy the peaceful fruit of realistic expectations.

God never gives us a calling without providing all we need to get it done, and that includes time and emotional capacity. If we aren't able to get it done, despite our best efforts, then He has a different plan in mind—perhaps a different person or a different time. Let's listen when the Holy Spirit gently calls us to set certain things aside and trust that He has them in His control.

Reflect

Is there some way in which you are limping along, trying to do it all, and not getting anything done well? In what way might you need to pull yourself off the field for a time, and trust God with the results?

Notes

"STRENGTH OF MY HEART, I NEED NOT FAIL, NOT MIND TO FEAR BUT TO OBEY, WITH SUCH A LEADER, WHO COULD QUAIL? THOU ART AS THOU WERT YESTERDAY. STRENGTH OF MY HEART, I REST IN THEE, FULFILL THY PURPOSES THROUGH ME."

— Amy Carmichael

Day 38

For this world is not our permanent home; we are looking forward to a home yet to come. Therefore, let us offer through Jesus a continual sacrifice of praise to God, proclaiming our allegiance to his name.
— Hebrews 13:14-15

Believing the Best in the Worst

I was worried about my 14-year-old son. At age 11 he was diagnosed with epilepsy, and although his physical seizures were thankfully controlled by medication, his abnormal neurological activity was another matter. No matter what medications his neurologists tried, he had brain "spikes" that interfered with his ability to learn, to follow a group conversation, and to be the charming class clown he had been before. He worked so hard to overcome his challenges and got D's anyway.

As a mom, I shed many tears. My worries for him and his future loomed so large. Can you relate? Is there something about which you silently cry, *Lord, how could you let this happen?*

I'll tell you when my perspective changed: when I noticed the inexplicable joy apparent in the lives of those who had it far worse. The smiling dad pushing his wheelchair-bound, special-needs son. The girl with no hair from chemo—and her trusting parents. The mom who lost her son to suicide, who nevertheless trusted that God would somehow, some way, work all things together for good.

A friend of mine recently reconnected with a high school classmate, Gloria, who had developed a neurological condition that left her unable to move, speak, or breathe on her own. My friend was

Shift Your Perspective

astonished to see Gloria's bright, smiling, joyful blue eyes behind the breathing mask.

Gloria can only communicate by moving her eyes to spell out words. It's a lot of work, so all her words are intentional. And she isn't easily annoyed with petty things. To the contrary, she is joyful, never complains, and has no hint of self-pity. She conveys only praise and worship for her Creator and Savior, Jesus Christ.

"How do you do it?" my friend asked in amazement.

Gloria spelled this out: "He has never failed me. He has met every need I have ever had." She was looking through her difficult circumstances to God, and focusing on the wonder of who He is.

Our God loves us. He will not always take us out of our circumstances, but He will always meet our needs in those circumstances. To believe and trust in Him, to be intentionally grateful even in legitimately difficult times, is one of the highest forms of praise and thanksgiving. It produces joy. Look for how He always meets your needs, rest in Him, and watch His joy consume your anxiety.

Reflect

Is worry or self-pity about any of your current circumstances overriding intentional gratitude? Today, share with someone or write in your journal at least three things you are grateful to God for in those trying circumstances.

Notes

_____

_____

_____

_____

_____

_____

_____

_____

"SPEAK GOD'S WORD OVER YOURSELF UNTIL YOU'VE CHANGED YOUR OWN MIND."

— Priscilla Shirer

All the days of the afflicted are bad,
But a cheerful heart has a continual feast.
— Proverbs 15:15, NASB

Not Just an Attitude

During one of my research studies, I learned how important it is for life and relationships for people to be able to "look on the bright side" of things. I discovered that temperament and personality type do not determine cheerfulness. In fact, several of my study participants described themselves as "recovering pessimists." The key to living a cheerful life is choosing gratitude.

Transforming gratitude chooses to view the glass as half full. When your son unpacks his backpack in the middle of the kitchen table just minutes before dinner, you say how glad you are to see that he's not putting off studying until bedtime—and resist asking if he would like the family to eat on the floor while he does his homework.

Transforming gratitude chooses to intentionally repeat the positive rather than the negative. When someone asks how your holiday break was, you talk about the great food, fun, and family, and completely skip over the complaining cousin you had to endure for a week.

Transforming gratitude chooses to focus on the one piece of good news amidst a cluster of bad. Your flight for the business trip was delayed two hours, the toddler in the next seat spilled his mom's coffee on you, and your rental car wasn't ready. But when your boyfriend

asks how your trip is going, you tell him you landed safely and the view is beautiful, mentioning nothing of the hassles in getting there.

Transforming gratitude chooses to believe the best about someone when we know the worst about them. Yes, your college student has overdrawn their account multiple times, but you tell her how proud you are of her hard work, and you continue to send her money for food and toiletries, trusting that eventually she will learn to manage better.

Transforming gratitude chooses to overlook minor offenses rather than magnify them. When your husband reaches up to open the door of the church to usher you in for a friend's wedding, and his arm bumps your head and knocks your hair clip out, you smile and excuse yourself to fix it rather than heaving an exasperated sigh.

Transforming gratitude is not always easy, but it is a choice any of us can make. The beautiful irony is that when we work to practice this choice, we discover that we don't have to work hard at cheerfulness and joy in life because now they come much more naturally.

Reflect

Which of the gratitude actions mentioned here would serve you well right now? Identify one, write it down, and resolve to pray about and practice it.

Notes

_____

_____

_____

_____

_____

_____

_____

"NEGATIVE PEOPLE NEED DRAMA LIKE OXYGEN. STAY POSITIVE, IT'LL TAKE THEIR BREATH AWAY."

— Tony Gaskins

*By wisdom a house is built, and through understanding
it is established; through knowledge its rooms are filled
with rare and beautiful treasures.*
— *Proverbs 24:3-4, NIV*

What Fills Your Home with Delight

I looked at Jeff, perplexed. After an evening of laughter, prayer, and Bible study, our small group was wrapping up. I had been joking around with my husband when he suddenly shut down. Jeff had told the group, "Well, we've got to get home. The kitchen sink broke, and I have to figure out how to fix it." I laughed. "Oh good grief, remember that time you broke the dishwasher trying to fix it? We had water all over our floor! Just call the plumber!"

His lighthearted expression disappeared. He covered well, but I could tell he was upset. In the stony silence on the way home, I began prodding. "What's wrong? Seriously, you're mad about that? Come on, I was just teasing."

Like many of us, I had no idea how clueless I was. We had a good marriage, but plenty of heartache too. And I didn't realize just how much of that heartache was caused by my own blindness. I looked at my strong, confident, capable husband—and had no idea how much self-doubt he had inside. I didn't know that he, like most men, carried around both a deep desire to provide for and protect his family (including being able to fix the kitchen sink!), and a deep vulnerability

about whether he measured up. I didn't know just how much he was longing for affirmation from his wife. I deeply loved and appreciated my husband, and I had no idea that every day I did things that sent the opposite message. It wasn't until later, when I surveyed so many men for *For Women Only,* that I began to wake up.

Ladies, so often, we have no idea how much we don't know about the key people in our lives . . . or the vast, profound difference we'll see in the relationship (and our own hearts!) once our eyes are opened.

In Proverbs, King Solomon paints a picture of how important wisdom and understanding are for building a home. But what is in your home? Are the rooms filled with stress, unhappiness, and conflict? Or is there joy around every corner? Is there companionship in the kitchen, cooperation in the playroom, and delight in the bedroom? God says that right knowledge—truly grasping the inner heart of the other person and what they most need (and avoiding what most hurts them)—is what fills our home with those rare and precious treasures.

Reflect

Among the key people you care about, do you sometimes find yourself confused about why something you did or said made them upset? Are you unsure how to please them? What book, article, or other resource could help you understand this person and gain the knowledge you need?

Notes

_____

_____

_____

_____

_____

_____

_____

_____

_____

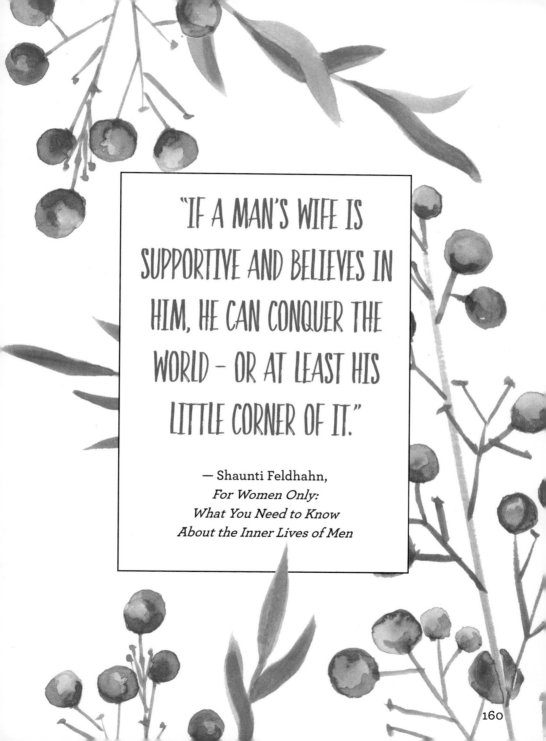

"IF A MAN'S WIFE IS SUPPORTIVE AND BELIEVES IN HIM, HE CAN CONQUER THE WORLD – OR AT LEAST HIS LITTLE CORNER OF IT."

— Shaunti Feldhahn,
For Women Only:
What You Need to Know
About the Inner Lives of Men

*The heavens declare the glory of God; the skies proclaim
the work of his hands. Day after day they pour forth
speech; night after night they reveal knowledge.*
— Psalm 19:1-4, NIV

Did You Notice?

How do we know God is listening when we cry to Him? Well, we might feel His peace. We might see a phrase in the Bible that jumps out at us. We might see Him moving in our circumstances. Or we might cross paths with one of His earthly angels—a person put in our lives for His specific purpose.

Years ago, I talked about this at length with a dear friend who was new to faith and struggled to see God in her daily life. We talked about how, when her heart felt heavy, she should slow down and just take notice of God at work. She later moved and we lost touch, until recently when I found a note from her in my inbox.

Circumstances had placed my friend and her family in a dire financial situation. Like many of us, she was feeling overwhelmed, desperate, and spiritually deserted. She was so weighed down that she couldn't see the way back up.

My friend tearfully pleaded with God for help. Suddenly, what came to mind was our talk from so many years ago. She made the deliberate decision to slow down and notice. She noticed the smile from her neighbor; the hug from a toddler whose ball she retrieved; the look of love from her husband across the room. She suddenly felt God's love surrounding her and sent Him silent thanks for not abandoning her.

Days later, a financial opportunity presented itself. It wasn't a long-term answer, but it provided just what their family needed for that moment. It was an outstretched hand leading her back into the light. She and her husband gradually dug themselves out from under their financial weight.

Some time later, they reflected on how they had managed to pull through. Her husband thought it was lucky, stumbling upon that timely opportunity that started them on the road back. My friend fervently disagreed. "I have come to believe that luck is nothing more than the hand of God," she said. "That was our darkest moment. And that was when He showed His love and answered my anguished prayers. He provided just what we needed, just when we needed it."

Friends, God is always there, and always moving, it's just that we don't always notice. Our lives will change forever once we resolve to not miss God's hand in our ascent from the darkness.

Reflect

Has God used someone to impact your direction when you were questioning? Have you received a smile from a stranger just when you needed it? Ever considered that your desire to smile at a stranger might be God using you to lighten that person's day? "Notice" Him by jotting down a few examples.

Notes

_____

_____

_____

_____

_____

_____

_____

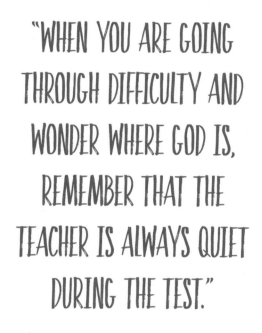

"WHEN YOU ARE GOING THROUGH DIFFICULTY AND WONDER WHERE GOD IS, REMEMBER THAT THE TEACHER IS ALWAYS QUIET DURING THE TEST."

—Author Unknown.
Referenced in the movie
God's Not Dead 2

Jesus said, "Everything is possible for one who believes."
Immediately the boy's father exclaimed,
"I do believe; help me overcome my unbelief!"
— Mark 9:23-24, NIV

Help My Unbelief

Recently, a guest preacher at our church proclaimed this about God's promises in the Bible: "I sincerely, deeply, strongly believe all of God's promises. Until I don't." The whole congregation started laughing. Who doesn't feel that way sometimes?

That is why I love the story of the father who comes to Jesus because his son is oppressed by an evil spirit and suffers from dangerous seizures. This desperate dad says, essentially, "If you can do anything, please do it!" And Jesus echoes, "If I can?" When He reassures the dad that everything is possible for those who believe, the dad cries out that he does believe—and also needs help because he doesn't!

Friends, as one who is both fully God and fully human, Jesus is not shocked by our human doubt. He understands. We can be vulnerable enough to cry out our belief in Him while at the same time begging for increased faith. Especially in our most desperate moments.

A few years ago, a friend's son was diagnosed with a rare genetic disorder. Devastated, she couldn't stop herself from researching the potential suffering they could expect over his lifetime. How she wished a doctor would give her this promise: "Everything will turn out just the way you want it to." But in a broken world, that's not how

life works—and it isn't how God works either. Sometimes we get that diagnosis. Sometimes a husband leaves, or a beloved family member dies too early. Sometimes our future is uncertain and frightening.

To counter her fear, my friend wrote down and reminded herself of these promises, which *are* how God works: God would never leave or forsake her family and her son (Deuteronomy 31:6). They would often not understand why something hard was happening, because God's ways are higher than ours (Isaiah 55:8-9). Yet God had plans for her son, to ultimately prosper and not harm him (Jeremiah 29:11). Their earthly sufferings would seem light and momentary compared to the glory to come (Romans 8:18; 2 Corinthians 4:17). Most of all, she clung to Proverbs 3:5-6: "Trust in the LORD with all your heart; do not depend on your own understanding. Seek his will in all you do, and he will show you which path to take."

When we struggle with worry, let's cling to these promises. And when we can't do even that, let's beg God to help our unbelief. He will.

Reflect

What is one area in your life where you want to believe
God is with you and has your best interests at heart,
but you're still struggling? Come to Jesus, affirm your
belief in Him, and ask Him to help your unbelief.

Notes

_____

_____

_____

_____

_____

_____

_____

_____

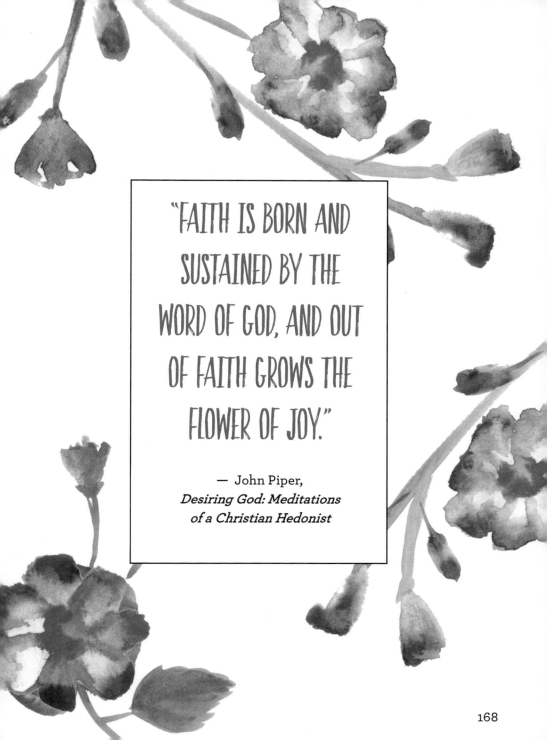

"FAITH IS BORN AND SUSTAINED BY THE WORD OF GOD, AND OUT OF FAITH GROWS THE FLOWER OF JOY."

— John Piper,
Desiring God: Meditations of a Christian Hedonist

168

In Him you have been made complete.
— Colossians 2:10, NASB

If Only We Would Look to Christ

I'd feel better about myself if only XYZ was different.

Do you ever think that? Marie did. She was living the "if only" life, in fact. As a single woman, she flitted from guy to guy, career to career, activity to activity. Nothing seemed to fit. If only she could find the perfect man, she would be happy. If only she had a better job, she would feel fulfilled. Then she met and married a wonderful man—and was surprised that the "if onlys" stayed. If only they had a better house or could make more money. If only she could have children. Soon she had a beautiful baby in her arms, but still felt that emptiness. She filled up her schedule with exciting activities, but something was still missing, something that would make her feel better about herself.

Something was missing, but it wasn't what she thought. She was missing the fulfillment that can only come from one thing: the deep realization that we have been created by a loving God to be who we are, with His purpose for our lives—and with a void that can only be filled by Him.

As women, we often use busyness as a source of fulfillment or to feel better about ourselves. If I have someone who loves me, whom I

spend time with (husband, children, or friends), it shows I belong and am lovable. If I have a busy job where people depend on me, it shows I am worth something. When my schedule is stretched, it shows I'm needed. I feel good about myself . . . for a while.

When we do this, we are looking for fulfillment in the wrong places. We need to shift our gaze and look up—to our Savior who has already completed us and to our God who claims us as His "dearly beloved children."

Let that sink in. We are complete in Christ. When we feel bad—not beautiful, not loved, not enough—and are tempted to look around for fulfillment, let's instead choose to stop and look up to our Savior. Let's ask Him to fill those longings in our hearts, and rest as He does just that.

Jesus is always waiting for us to turn to Him because He knows that He alone can satisfy our longings and fully complete us in every way.

Reflect

How are you looking to your activities, busyness, relationships, or job to complete and fulfill you? How will you choose to handle the situations that arise today?

Notes

_____

_____

_____

_____

_____

_____

_____

_____

"GOD IS STILL AT WORK,
EVEN WHEN WE'RE NOT."

— Kathi Lipp,
*Overwhelmed: How to Quiet the
Chaos and Restore Your Sanity*

Beware of practicing your righteousness before
men to be noticed by them; otherwise you have
no reward with your Father who is in heaven.
— *Matthew 6:1, NASB*

Serving the Joneses

"My skirt hasn't hit my fanny all day" is an old Southern expression that describes our modern-day busyness. Some are trying to "keep up with the Joneses," but many of us have a different problem. We've fallen into the more noble pursuit of "serving the Joneses" or "pleasing the Joneses," because we subconsciously want to feel good about what we're doing or are looking for accolades.

Suppose you committed a few weeks back to bring dinner to a friend after surgery. Now the day is here—along with twenty other things to do. Let's evaluate some common internal dialogue, along with some truths that we often don't say.

> I decided to bring Sonya my special, complicated chicken casserole, which her kids love. *(And, if I'm honest, I'm proud of it and I love their reactions.)* I can't just buy frozen chicken tenders! *(Are those the only two choices? What about simple crock-pot chicken?)* I know I've been pushing off reading Dan's client proposal that he asked for my feedback on last week, and Grammie needs her flu shot, and I've got to get the summer camp registrations done or the kids' favorite spots will be taken. *(But those things are so mundane and I don't get cheers for it—even*

though those are the people I'm called to serve first.) But after all, if I don't get that meal made, Sonya's family will be so disappointed *(self-induced drama)*, and they won't have anything to eat. *(Exaggeration—they will have something, but it will be less than my "Martha Stewart" best.)*

So easily, our good calling to serve others becomes a self-induced expectation that takes us away from our more core calling to serve our family and others out of Christlike love. It feels good to be appreciated by the grateful friend. The everyday residents of our home may just shrug and smile—or keep watching TV. We can even become resentful when we expect appreciation that we don't get.

But even when a husband or kids (or boss or customers) don't show appreciation for our service, the One who draped His waist with a towel to wash His disciples' feet does see. Out of gratitude for what He has done for us, let us love and serve those He has called us to and wait for our reward in heaven.

Reflect

What are some clues that you are expecting recognition
and/or gratitude rather than serving from love? If God
cares most about attitude and motive, which of your
acts of service do you think most please Him?

Notes

"WE MUST NOT CONFUSE THE COMMAND TO LOVE WITH THE DISEASE TO PLEASE."

— Lysa TerKeurst

But who can discern their own errors? Forgive my hidden faults.
— *Psalm 19:12*

What Is Wrong with Me?

There was a time when my children were young that I found myself very off-balance. As my ministry grew, I started to leave them at preschool for a few extra hours each day . . . then longer . . . then longer. Eventually, I found myself irritated at having to knock off work to go pick them up by the time the preschool closed at 6 p.m.! What was wrong with me?

Desperate, I asked God to shine a light on what was going on inside. Soon I saw the ugly truth: I was feeling more fulfilled, equipped, and energized to be a speaker and author to thousands than a mother to two. "What do I do?" I asked God, through tears. And the quiet answer came: *Pick them up at 3 p.m.*

"But, Lord," I argued, "There are a lot of days that I have deadlines beyond that—"

Pick them up at 3 p.m.

Once I set aside the urgent for the important and obeyed God's strict deadline, something amazing happened: I started to want to be with my kids more. I was spending more time with them, so I started to miss them when we weren't together.

Connect with God

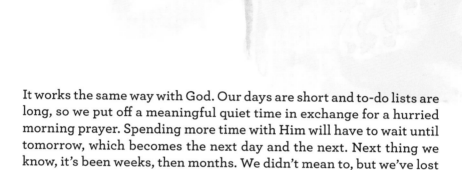

It works the same way with God. Our days are short and to-do lists are long, so we put off a meaningful quiet time in exchange for a hurried morning prayer. Spending more time with Him will have to wait until tomorrow, which becomes the next day and the next. Next thing we know, it's been weeks, then months. We didn't mean to, but we've lost our connection and the relationship is distant.

Yet we desperately need to be in touch with God, both out of love for Him and His love for us. The more distant we get, the more His light becomes unable to reach the dark corners of our hearts. We don't see the ways we are out of balance, stubborn, prideful, or unkind. And the more distant we get, the more unlikely it is that we'll see His light on the path He wants us to follow out of the darkness.

Tim Keller gives my favorite description of the gospel: We are more sinful and flawed than we ever dared believe, yet more loved and accepted than we ever dared hope. Let's give our Lord the time to illuminate our flaws and show us the path to becoming women who look more like Him.

Reflect

Over these last few weeks, how have you been doing at
regularly connecting with God in a meaningful way?
Go to God now and ask Him to show you what one or two
"hidden faults" He wants you to see and work on in your life.

Notes

_____

_____

_____

_____

_____

_____

_____

_____

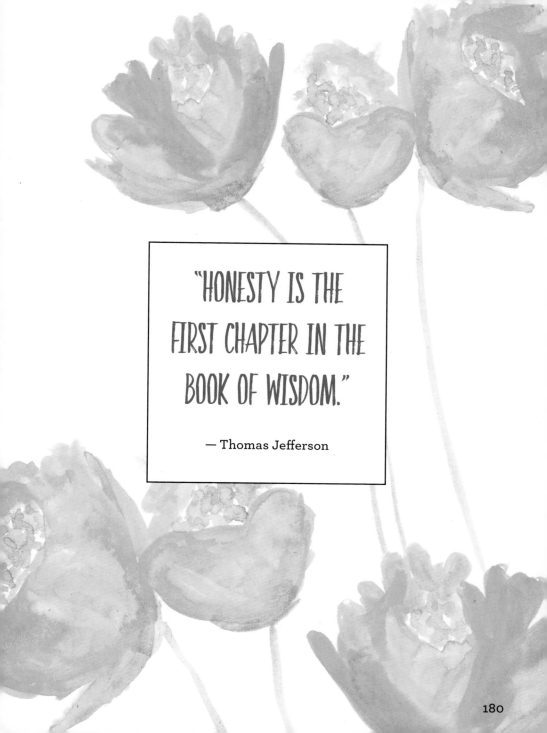

"HONESTY IS THE
FIRST CHAPTER IN THE
BOOK OF WISDOM."

— Thomas Jefferson

Pay careful attention to your own work, for then you will get the satisfaction of a job well done, and you won't need to compare your-self to anyone else. For we are each responsible for our own conduct.
— Galatians 6:4-5

True Satisfaction

When we think about comparing ourselves with others, we assume that "comparisons" build envy or dissatisfaction. And they do, of course. But they can also feed pride. What a toxic mix!

As a student at a highly competitive college, I sometimes found myself caught in that trap. I was proud to be at this great school but at the same time wished I was beautiful and popular like certain classmates. I was privately smug when I got a great internship but also deeply annoyed by others who did less work but got better grades.

Later, as an analyst on Wall Street, the comparisons morphed into *Why was she recognized more for that initiative, when I did more work?* Same song. Different verse. Then after six months leading a different organization, I added a new verse to that song: *How can they fire me? Don't they realize that I'm far more motivated than others, and was working under impossible conditions?*

With my pride deeply wounded, and lots of time suddenly on my hands, I evaluated myself. I'd been caught in the comparison game, envious of those who had what I wanted, and yet prideful in what I did have, as if it was all because of me. I didn't like what I saw in the mirror.

Ever been there? Maybe you're comparing yourself to that person on social media who's thin and well-dressed, with children who are always smiling . . . while you're in your pajamas at 2 p.m., refereeing three squabbling preschoolers. Maybe, like me, you've been fired or demoted from a job that you loved. Or perhaps you're secretly smug about your slim, well-toned body (um, what was I saying about being envious?) but jealous of your friend's strong, happy marriage.

We become alternately prideful and dissatisfied when we play the comparison game. Because that is the enemy's game, not God's.

God tells us that when we focus on what *we* can do instead of what others are doing, we will have great satisfaction, and we won't even need to compare ourselves. God made us unique, and He has a perfect plan for each of us because of our uniqueness. We must not trigger either pride or discouragement by looking at others. Let's accept how we each are made, fearfully and wonderfully, and embrace the plan that God has designed just for us.

Reflect

In what ways are you playing the comparison game? How is
it making you prideful? How is it making you dissatisfied?
And what does God want you to embrace about yourself today?

Notes

_____

_____

_____

_____

_____

_____

_____

_____

"WE HAVE A GOD WHO SAYS WE ARE ENOUGH. JUST AS WE ARE."

— Michele Cushatt

She opens her mouth in wisdom, And the
teaching of kindness is on her tongue.
— *Proverbs 31:26, NASB*

Treat Him Differently

A friend of mine was known for her funny, tell-it-like-it-is personality. Whether asking for career advice or her opinion on an outfit, everyone knew to be prepared for the response. Her wit made us laugh even as we winced. Somehow, her humor made it ok . . . most of the time.

Newly married to a wonderful man, she was stunned one day by his profound reply to a snippy remark. While Christmas shopping together, she was irritated when he willingly parked far away from the mall rather than circling to find a closer space. With some bite in her voice, she said, "You sure you want to park this far away? There might be some parking spots in Canada you haven't checked out."

He paused, turned toward her, and gently said, "You can't speak to me like that." My friend quickly replied, "But I speak to everyone like that!"

Her husband's reply is something we should all heed: "I know. But the one person you have to be different with is me."

Ladies, whether the man in your life is a husband, boyfriend, brother, or son, remember this key truth about men: for all their bravado, they are vulnerable inside. They have a deep self-doubt: Am I good enough? Do I measure up?

Create Life-Giving Relationships

To the degree you have any tensions or conflict in that relationship, it is very likely those tensions come from forgetting that your man has that fear. You have a great ability to either dispel or confirm it.

If God's plan for you includes marriage, He has given you a very special and delicate gift. As the years pass, we often forget the intricate and vulnerable heart of our man. We see him daily, we know his strengths and imperfections, and we may begin to take him for granted. Because we feel safe with him, we may not realize that we're speaking to him in a tone we would never even use with a friend. Our words tear him down.

The solution is the sage advice from my friend's husband: Treat him differently. Build him up and encourage him. Help him to see his great worth in your eyes. If you have issues to raise, do it in a way that honors his tender heart. And as you take care with this delicate, special relationship, you'll see it shine like gold.

Reflect

Do your words toward the important man (or boy) in your life build him up? tear him down? both? What one or two things can you do in the short-term to build a positive habit? Ask God to show you when you revert to old habits.

Notes

_____

_____

_____

_____

_____

_____

_____

_____

"LORD, MAKE ME AN INSTRUMENT OF THY PEACE. WHERE THERE IS HATRED, LET ME SOW LOVE."

— Francis of Assisi

*If we confess our sins to him, he is faithful and just to
forgive us our sins and to cleanse us from all wickedness.*
— 1 John 1:9

Come into the Light

Many times we try to hide something: a secret sin, guilt from our past, the fact that we're having marriage troubles, the worry about our preteen son's fascination with porn. We think our close friends wouldn't understand. We don't want to look like we're in need. Whatever the situation, when we are too prideful to be transparent and choose instead to hide anything important from God and from others whom He has put in our life to help, it will cause stress.

I recently heard a story about a man who wed his beautiful bride, and then immediately realized that something just wasn't right in his marriage. There was a barrier between his wife and him, and he couldn't figure out what it was. The more he prayed, the more it seemed as if there was a spiritual wall between them.

Fast forward several years into their marriage. One Sunday morning, after hearing a sermon on sin, this man's wife burst into tears and went forward for prayer. She confessed to God and to her husband a sin of betrayal she had committed before they were married. Their entire married life she felt she had been living a lie. She thought that if she had admitted her sin to her husband, he would have never married her. She lived in fear of her marriage falling apart and was not transparent before her husband, or even before God.

This young woman's lack of transparency was holding her back from experiencing all that God intended her marriage to be. The act of holding back had created the very types of problems she was worried would come if she shared what was really going on. The worry, fear, and stress of her sin had been plaguing her for years, to the point of causing physical symptoms. Her confession was an answer to prayer for her husband. He forgave her, and their marriage finally began to blossom.

Ever since God created human beings, the tendency to sin and to hide has produced barriers between us and our Creator—and between us and the people around us. When we are keeping anything hidden in the darkness, especially unconfessed sin, we cannot live the authentic, abundant, joyful life God wants us to have. God is faithful to forgive and restore us if we set aside our pride and come into the light.

Reflect

Are you feeling as if there is a barrier between you and
God and/or others? Is there something you need to repent
of before the Lord or others in your life? Is there something
you're keeping in the darkness? Bring it before God today,
and ask Him for help in bringing it into the light.

Notes

"NEVER BE AFRAID TO
TRUST AN UNKNOWN
FUTURE TO A KNOWN GOD."

— Corrie Ten Boom

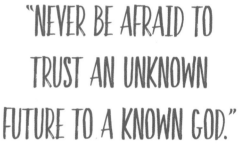

Have I not commanded you? Be strong and courageous.
Do not be afraid; do not be discouraged, for the Lord
your God will be with you wherever you go.
— Joshua 1:9, NIV

Being a Fearless Daughter

Not long ago, I watched a young girl climb to the very top of the neighborhood jungle gym beside our home. My heart stopped for a second as she perched for a leap. She cried, "Daddy!" and as a man nearby swung around to look at her, she launched herself into the blue. He raced forward and caught her. She was laughing in delight, but I think his heart had stopped for a second, just like mine.

At first, I found myself mentally wagging a finger at the child's foolishness. But I suddenly realized: that is exactly how trusting we should be with our heavenly Father. We are supposed to be like that young girl, who believed so fully in her father that she was oblivious to repercussions and thus courageous enough to take chances (Matthew 18:3). Children don't fear the worst; instead they naively trust that nothing bad will happen.

This kind of childlike innocence is what enables us to take chances. To voice an opinion without fear of judgment. To talk about Jesus without worrying about what others might think.

Or maybe your fear is less about what others think of you and more about your ability to get it all done. Maybe your problem (and mine, too!) is being unwilling to set aside the urgent for the important.

To leave the big report on our desk and spend time with a husband who deeply needs our attention, even if we're not sure how that work deadline is going to be met.

Somewhere in the journey of life, fearlessness gets replaced by worry. The more hectic and rushed our lives become, the more we play it safe, because when we are overwhelmed and tired, we take the path of least resistance. We shy away from conflict in hopes of avoiding trouble. Or we allow our fear of missing an immediate deadline (our report) to keep us from attending to something that is far, far more important for our whole life (our marriage).

What if we could let go of our inhibitions, take more risks, and trust God? We might discover that whether we are voicing an opinion, talking about Jesus, or deciding to set aside the urgent for the important, He is there. Our heavenly Father is just waiting for us to trust Him and fearlessly climb that jungle gym, confident that when we leap, He will be there with arms wide open.

Reflect

In what areas do you hold back out of fear? Have you ever stopped yourself from sharing your true thoughts or your faith for fear of being viewed negatively? Or sacrificed the important for the urgent? What is one thing that you can do differently for the next few weeks that would build a different habit?

Notes

_____

_____

_____

_____

_____

_____

_____

_____

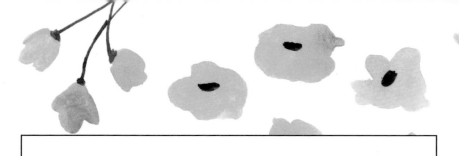

"BECOME A WORRY-SLAPPER. TREAT FRETS LIKE MOSQUITOES. DO YOU PROCRASTINATE WHEN A BLOODSUCKING BUG LIGHTS ON YOUR SKIN? 'I'LL TAKE CARE OF IT IN A MOMENT.' OF COURSE YOU DON'T! YOU GIVE THE CRITTER THE SLAP IT DESERVES. BE EQUALLY DECISIVE WITH ANXIETY."

— Max Lucado

That is why I tell you not to worry about everyday life—whether you have enough food and drink, or enough clothes to wear . . . Look at the birds. They don't plant or harvest or store food in barns, for your heavenly Father feeds them. And aren't you far more valuable to him than they are? . . . [Y]our heavenly Father already knows all your needs. Seek the Kingdom of God above all else, and live righteously, and he will give you everything you need."
—*Matthew 6:25-26, 32-33*

Contentment in All Circumstances

My friend went back into the workforce once her kids were in school. She was thrilled to be offered a good paying job working for some casual friends, and her family enjoyed the benefits of the extra income. But as she advanced, she discovered that the inner workings of the company were less than ethical. She raised her concerns and was told, "This is how it is with business." She knew in her heart she could not continue working there, so she turned in her resignation.

Her family instantly lost one-third of their income. They weren't wealthy; her income had freed them from worrying if they would be able to afford an unexpected trip to the pediatrician or car repair. Now, it was a daily struggle to make ends meet. My friend really struggled with resentment and fear, but she knew she needed to develop contentment instead.

Have you ever been there? I sure have. I look at the bank balance and wonder, *How are we going to pay the phone bill?* I look at the upcoming vacation weekend from school and think, *I wish we could afford to go to the beach.* I look at my son who struggles with learning and think, *I wish he didn't have to work so hard.*

My friend found that there was only one answer: to take her eyes off what she didn't have, thank God for what she did have, and honor Him in all of it. She started a gratitude journal. Each day she would write, "Today we have shelter over our heads. We have food to eat. We have clothes to wear. We have a vehicle that gets us where we need to go." She started with the basics. Like the apostle Paul, they had everything they really needed.

Most importantly, they had their faith. Their circumstances may have changed, but their God hadn't. God provided food for the birds and apparel for the flowers, and God would also provide for them. By continually reminding herself that God really was with them, my friend found contentment.

Circumstances in our lives will change, but God never will. He has promised to provide for us just as any good parent provides for his or her children. The key is to be content with what God provides, knowing that regardless of our circumstances we are not alone.

Reflect

In what area are you struggling with contentment? Take your eyes off those things today, and instead look at Him. Make a long list of everything God has given you . . . and thank Him for all of it.

Notes

_____

_____

_____

_____

_____

_____

_____

_____

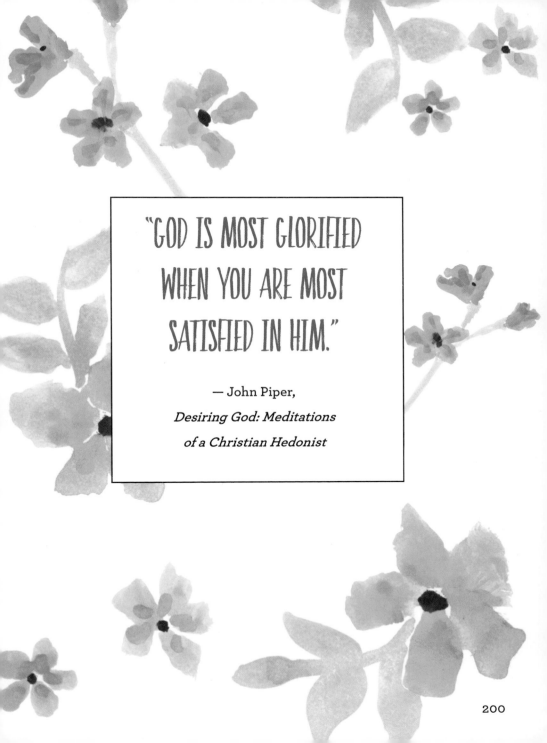

"GOD IS MOST GLORIFIED
WHEN YOU ARE MOST
SATISFIED IN HIM."

— John Piper,
Desiring God: Meditations
of a Christian Hedonist

*Why do you look at the speck of sawdust in your brother's eye
and pay no attention to the plank in your own eye? How can
you say to Your brother, "Let me take the speck out of your eye,"
when all the time there is a plank in your own eye? You hypocrite,
first take the plank out of your own eye, and then you will see
clearly to remove the speck from your brother's eye.*
— *Matthew 7:3-5, NIV*

Don't Play That Game

One of my favorite research projects was studying very happily married couples to figure out what they did differently. Whether we are married, dating, or single, we can learn from them about building great relationships.

As I spoke with couples who had experienced a radical change for the better in their marriage, I was struck by a common thread: They had purposefully stopped the "If you" game. You know the one—"Well, I'll change if you do"; "If you get an evening with the boys, I get one with the girls"; "I'd stop talking to my mom so much if you were more attentive." They often found this change was needed in many areas of life. ("If you clean up your cubicle, maybe I'll turn down my music.")

Ironically, we usually start the "If you" game because we want to be happier. And yet there are few things more likely to make us miserable—or more blind to the beauty that could arise in the relationship if we were only willing to look at ourselves.

One woman told me how she learned this lesson as a young newlywed. Early on, it seemed she was always angry. Her relationship with her husband felt more like a chess game than a partnership. She'd make a move and watch for what his next move would be. "As soon as he starts doing X, then I'll do Y" or "He's going to have to apologize first." She got more and more frustrated as she felt he never made the right move. More often than not, she said, he would make no move at all.

Suddenly, she realized: her husband was oblivious to the game! It was a game she was playing with no other players.

Embarrassed, she felt God calling her out on her game-playing. She was setting herself up to be frustrated, essentially looking for her husband to let her down or fail. And she was completely ignoring the ways she could be frustrating to her husband. She realized that her husband was not constantly pointing out those things. He certainly was not perfect, but he was not saying, "If you." Whenever she would begin to think, "Well, when he does . . ." she felt the Holy Spirit whisper "game playing!" Eventually, God trained her to recognize and stop those thoughts before they even started. When she stopped game playing, their marriage won.

Reflect

How might you be causing your own stress by playing
the "if you" game? What "splinter" is God trying to
point out in your own eye, and how can you remove it?

Notes

_____

_____

_____

_____

_____

_____

_____

_____

"YOU CAN'T LOSE IF YOU DON'T PLAY THE GAME."

– William Shakespeare

Romeo and Juliet (modern translation) , Act 1, Scene 4, page 2

Whatever you give is acceptable if you give it eagerly. And
give according to what you have, not what you don't have.
— *2 Corinthians 8:12*

Bring Your Gift

I returned home from an exhausting trip at about 4 p.m. I wearily lugged my suitcase inside, looked at my calendar—and panicked! I had totally forgotten that, weeks before, I had signed up to bring a meal that night to a family whose mom had just had surgery. I peered in our sadly neglected refrigerator and thought, *How am I going to make dinner with that?* It felt like one of those game shows where one is challenged to feed a family of four with one egg, a droopy celery stalk, and a jar of olives.

I hastily found some frozen meatballs, cooked them with a jar of sauce I spotted far back on a shelf, heated up frozen green beans, peeled a big bowl of oranges, filched a bag of chips from the kids' junk-food stash, and raced to deliver the meal, praying that it wouldn't taste as inadequate as it seemed.

The next day, the mom called to tell me her family had raved about the meatballs! I was relieved, but surprised. It was such a desperate offering, I knew the only reason for the raves was God's blessing on the gift. It suddenly reminded me of the time when ten thousand or more people were listening to Jesus preach, and He suddenly turned to His disciples and said, "feed them." The disciples were incredulous.

A young boy appeared with his meager lunch—a few loaves of bread and a few fish. The disciples looked in their proverbial refrigerator and said, "Um, Jesus, there's no way we can feed all these people with a little bread and fish. Time to send everyone for Chinese food!"

But Jesus blessed the gift. The massive crowd was fed with leftovers running over.

This boy who offered his lunch was certainly not the only one in the crowd who had brought food. But everyone else thought what we would probably think in such a situation: What could be done with my tiny portion? What difference would this make? The boy didn't let those thoughts stop him. He put aside any embarrassment or timidity, pushed through the thronging crowd, and gave Jesus what he had.

And look what Jesus did with it. A little gift turns into one of the biggest miracles in the Bible. Friends, let's not hang back and miss the blessing. God will use any gift we bring, when we trust He will use it for His glory.

Reflect

What is something you feel God wants you to bring to Him, even if it seems like an inadequate gift? How can you view it in the light of the boy and his loaves and fishes—can you trust God to take what you have to offer and bless it beyond what you can imagine?

Notes

"THE GROWING GOOD OF THE WORLD IS PARTLY DEPENDENT ON UNHISTORIC ACTS; AND THAT THINGS ARE NOT SO ILL WITH YOU AND ME AS THEY MIGHT HAVE BEEN, IS HALF OWING TO THE NUMBER WHO LIVED FAITHFULLY A HIDDEN LIFE, AND REST IN UNVISITED TOMBS."

— Mary Ann Evans

(pen name: George Eliot), Middlemarch

*Like a parent feels compassion for their children—that's how
the Lord feels compassion for those who honor him. Because
God knows how we're made, God remembers we're just dust.*
— Psalm 103:13-14, CEB

Running in the Right Direction

A woman shared an all-too-familiar story. Her day had gone well. She'd managed to get some quiet time with the Lord before her children got off the bus. She felt calm, serene, and ready for whatever the evening held.

Then the children ran in and chaos erupted. Arguments, fighting, backbiting. There was even a full-blown tantrum ... and it wasn't from the kids. This mom felt lower than low. How soon she'd forgotten. How quickly she'd allowed her flesh to quench the peace and rest of the Spirit.

An angry word, an unkind thought, a thoughtless act. Do you ever find yourself hoping God isn't paying attention? When this happens, I want to run and hide. And as I do, it only gets worse.

Perhaps you're in a rough patch right now, and totally drained. Maybe you're appalled that even after 53 days of this devotional, your attitudes, words, and actions today weren't what you wanted them to be. Or maybe you're in a situation you never thought you'd be in, and you know it's because of your own choice to slide down that proverbial slippery slope—so knowing that God is aware of everything about you is not especially encouraging right now.

Rather than face it, you just want to run away.

Don't run. Or rather, run in the right direction: into the arms of a God who can handle it all. The Psalmist emphasizes that God has compassion on our weaknesses, just as a good father has compassion on his children. And having lived as a human, he knows our imperfections and innate humanness. He doesn't expect our life to be all puppies and rose petals.

God won't rain down fire and brimstone on your weaknesses. The Scriptures are full of examples of God embracing the exhausted, sorrowful wanderer. He longs to show you compassion.

I don't know where you find yourself as you read this, but God does. Come as you are, be transparent, and express your feelings to Him just as you would confide in a friend. As you give up the idea of presenting a "better self" to God, and instead come simply as you are, you will feel the relief of coming into the open—and knowing that God loves you anyway.

Reflect

Is there some way that you are running from God, or expecting Him to rain fire and brimstone on your weaknesses? How can you be honest and transparent with God so that you can experience His compassion?

Notes

_____

_____

_____

_____

_____

_____

_____

_____

"YOU CAN'T OUTRUN GRACE."

— Paul Tripp

Jonah video Bible Study

Day 54

Don't just pretend to love others. Really love them. . . . Be patient in trouble, and keep on praying. . . . Bless those who persecute you. Don't curse them; pray that God will bless them. Be happy with those who are happy, and weep with those who weep. Live in harmony with each other. . . . Do all that you can to live in peace with everyone.
— *Romans 12:9-18*

Respond in the Opposite Way

The most frequent command in the Bible is not what you might think. Commands to "love one another" are up there on the list, but the most common directive is some variation of "do not be afraid."

We don't really realize it, but we subconsciously feed, nurture, and accommodate fear—otherwise called "worry." For weeks, we've been looking at changing our perspective and taking thoughts captive. But do we still worry?

It's time to confront the ways we might be disobediently stoking our own anxieties. And one very common, unseen habit that is sure to feed worry is keeping track of what is fair or unfair—in other words, too fair to others and unfair toward you.

It is so easy to subconsciously tally up who said this or did that (I can't believe the boss remembered Mary in his thank-you speech and left my name out. I worked just as hard!). Who was next in line (it sure wasn't that rude man who cut in front of me) and who should wait their turn. Who owes or who paid and whether they paid their fair share.

Shift Your Perspective

I sure identified with the person who told me recently, "I realized that I am a 'high justice' sort of person!" And when we don't purposefully notice and confront those worried, snippy, or "high justice" thoughts, we allow them to rob us of kind ones—and kind actions.

God asks us to make a choice: to respond in the opposite way our hearts want to go. Think the best of others, not the worst. Let offenses go. Bless others, and do not curse.

Is your friend running late again? Counter the temptation to think, "She's so selfish; she only cares about her own schedule," and instead think, "I love her spontaneity and flexibility, and this is part of friendship with her. It is probably good for me to not be so tied to a clock." Your boss left your name out of his speech? Think, "I'm so glad Mary got recognized this time. She's been working so hard."

This mental discipline allows us to escape the exhaustion of subconscious mental scorekeeping and respond more like Christ, all at the same time.

Reflect

In the last few weeks, how did you sometimes think the worst instead of the best? What could you have thought instead? How can you do better going forward?

Notes

_____

_____

_____

_____

_____

_____

_____

_____

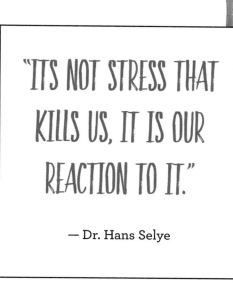

"ITS NOT STRESS THAT KILLS US, IT IS OUR REACTION TO IT."

— Dr. Hans Selye

All of you together are Christ's body, and each of you is a part of it.
— *1 Corinthians 12:27*

You Are Needed

Honda put out a remarkable commercial in 2003 called "Cog." A team disassembled a Honda Accord and put the individual parts into a domino-like setup, all starting with one simple, small cog. The cog slowly rolls down a decline, which then sets the chain reaction going—using car parts such as tires and pistons, windshield wipers, coils, and other doodads that most of us never even knew existed!

This 120 seconds of masterful planning ends with the key fob being pushed to close the trunk of a fully assembled Accord, and the phrase "Isn't it nice when things just work?"

There were many far simpler ways to close the trunk of the car. One person could've just pushed the key fob button. Done. But the point was not just to close the trunk: it was to get all the parts involved in a precise way. The big visible car parts and the small "what is that thing called?" parts were all necessary for the designer's ultimate purpose.

Life is kind of like that when you're a Christ follower. We all know God could take care of any issue, problem, or situation in the world. He could just "push the button" and do it all Himself. He doesn't have to use anyone in His divine plans.

But that's not how He works. Amazingly, our God has made every one of us important to His purposes. He has made each of us members of the body of Christ. And He uses us to accomplish His work.

Think about the times you felt a quiet nudge to offer compassion or encouragement, whether it was as simple as smiling at someone who looked like they were having a hard day or patiently holding the door for the elderly lady who was moving slowly. Maybe you felt like you should bring a meal to someone who was sick, or you realized you were in a position to be a friend to someone who was lonely or in need of advice. Perhaps you even felt a sobering sense that you had to lovingly challenge someone's destructive behavior.

Whatever it was, you were doing your part in God's purposeful display of His goodness to the world. So whenever you feel those nudges, listen. You may feel inconsequential, but step out anyway. God uses us all—small parts, big parts, and those parts in between—to accomplish His will.

Reflect

When have you felt a nudge to do something recently, even if it seemed minor? How was that action likely a part of God's plan?

Notes

_____

_____

_____

_____

_____

_____

_____

_____

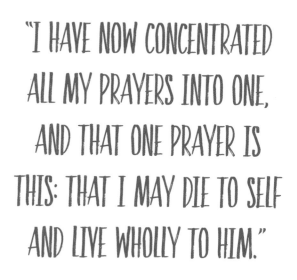

"I HAVE NOW CONCENTRATED ALL MY PRAYERS INTO ONE, AND THAT ONE PRAYER IS THIS: THAT I MAY DIE TO SELF AND LIVE WHOLLY TO HIM."

— Charles Spurgeon

You have searched me, Lord, and you know me. You know when
I sit and when I rise; you perceive my thoughts from afar. . . .
Before a word is on my tongue you, Lord, know it completely.
— Psalm 139:1-2, 4, NIV

Looking through the Shadows

The 2017 solar eclipse created quite a stir across the United States. In Atlanta, where we experienced almost complete totality (when the sun is fully obscured by the moon), it seemed no one was immune to the allure of watching the cosmic show. If we had lived thousands of years ago, I'm quite sure we would have intensely disliked experiencing sudden shadows and darkness! But in this case, we knew the cause of the darkness, and we welcomed it.

It's quite different when it applies to people, isn't it? When we see darkness and shadows come over those we love, it often causes deep frustration. Your teenage daughter has become a drama queen; you can hardly suggest anything without her erupting into tears. Your toddler is having tantrums in public. Your husband is increasingly withdrawn and grumpy. And now you're worried and grumpy yourself!

We become worried or frustrated because we don't know what is behind the darkness. The perpetual prickles of your teen daughter may signal a deep insecurity about the rejection of her group of friends. The increasingly disobedient toddler may be crying for more one-on-one time since you've been traveling so much for work. That distant husband may be anxious over an uncomfortable change at his

job and is worried that you don't understand his concern about how he will provide for the family.

My friend Megan has multiple kids, including a special-needs child who takes a lot of time. A few years back, she realized that another son, who is usually very happy, serves as the emotional barometer who signals when the family is getting out of balance. When he cries at the drop of a hat, that means too much time has been spent dealing with one child's school and doctor's appointments and not enough time loving on each one of her kids. Although she'd prefer to avoid that from the beginning, she has learned to be grateful for those ready tears rather than irritated with them because they signal what is in his heart—and cue her to schedule intentional time with each child to help restore closeness.

God knows every part of us, and He loves us exactly where we are. Part of the privilege of loving others is displaying that same type of love. That means looking past the shadows, past the behaviors, and reaching out to understand the true heart of those He has put in our lives.

Reflect

What is a behavior, attitude, or "shadow" you're seeing or dealing with right now in someone you love? Pray that as you move forward, God would open your eyes to the true heart of that person and give you wisdom on how to love them in the midst of their shadows.

Notes

_____

_____

_____

_____

_____

_____

_____

_____

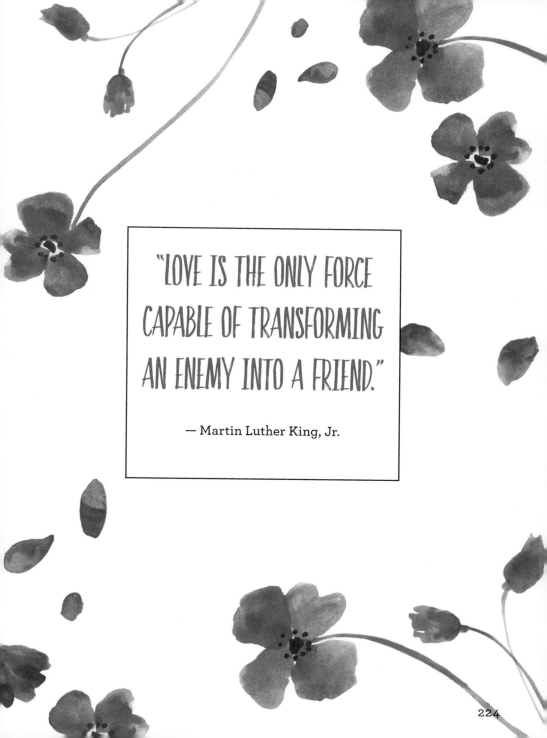

"LOVE IS THE ONLY FORCE CAPABLE OF TRANSFORMING AN ENEMY INTO A FRIEND."

— Martin Luther King, Jr.

But the Lord answered and said to her, "Martha, Martha, you are worried and bothered about so many things; but only one thing is necessary, for Mary has chosen the good part, which shall not be taken away from her."
— Luke 10:41-42, NASB

Choosing the Good Part

Over these many weeks together, we have seen how easy it is to be so driven by an endless series of back-to-back activities, meetings, or errands that we lose sight of what is truly necessary for the day. We know we need to shift our focus to someone or something else, but we are going so fast to get it all done that we don't *want* to shift directions!

We all have days like that. The problem we've been confronting, of course, is the habit of being controlled by our busyness. How can we avoid slipping back into old patterns? How do we ensure that we want to choose the "good part"?

One friend described the moment it finally clicked for her. She said, "I could tell my husband kept coming by my home office. Finally, I asked him if he needed something. He just wondered if I was going to watch TV with him. I told him, 'Not tonight, I'm working on a deadline.' Just like the night before and the night before that, and so on. I felt bad, but consoled myself that almost every night I made him dinner. I also made sure we had regular intimate time together. But suddenly, I realized: God was tugging on my heart! He wanted me to see the disappointment—time after time—in my husband's eyes. My

husband needed my companionship more than my projects did. . . . And God needed me to see that, to change my heart."

Whether it's a spouse, child, elderly parent, lonely neighbor, or some specific Kingdom calling, we need to be willing to let Jesus tug on our heart and show us the hearts of those around us. That is one of the key ways to redirect our focus from our to-do list to our most crucial callings.

When we ignore those heart tugs, we dive deeper and deeper into stress and weariness, because at that moment we are taking up the wrong yoke and laboring under it.

We need to trust that when we set aside the to-do compulsion and simply sit at the feet of Jesus, or by our lonely spouse and watch TV, our heavenly Father will help us meet or adjust the other priorities that loom so large. We need to trust that He'll give us a greater joy while also providing the way to accomplish what really needs to get done each day.

Reflect

Over the last few weeks, how has Jesus been tugging on your heart on behalf of those around you? Write those convictions down, and any actions you feel you're supposed to take now. Ask Him to help you not miss those heart tugs in the future.

Notes

_____

_____

_____

_____

_____

_____

_____

_____

"LOVE HAS NO AGE,
NO LIMIT; AND
NO DEATH."

— John Galsworthy

Do everything without complaining and arguing, so that no one can criticize you. Live clean, innocent lives as children of God, shining like bright lights in a world full of crooked and perverse people.
— *Philippians 2:14-15*

Replace Steam with Grace

I was helping a large corporation develop a women's leadership program when I met Nadia. Nadia was the highest-level female executive in the company and was deeply respected. She confided that she could trace her advancement to a change she'd made fifteen years before. Back then, she had a harsh, unkind boss, and she regularly vented about it to a female coworker. But even though the coworker was equally mistreated, she refused to join in.

Finally, she asked Nadia, "If you complain, does it change anything?" When Nadia admitted that it didn't actually change anything, her colleague shook her head. "You're wrong," she said. "It does change something. It changes you."

Nadia realized that complaining not only wasn't helping; it was hurting her. The more she voiced her frustrations, the more frustrations she saw to voice. And the more the missed the truly encouraging things around her.

We all have many reasons to grumble—probably even in the last few days! Maybe your colleague left you holding the bag, your husband caved to the kids after you begged him not to, or your teenager did not study for the SAT even after you paid for the prep class. Or maybe

(ahem) you're a women's speaker who bought a cute new outfit for a big women's event . . . and then drove into the church parking lot in pouring rain and realized you forgot to pack an umbrella.

When these annoyances arise, we think that venting is helpful because it "lets off steam" and keeps the kettle from exploding. But brain scientists have discovered that the opposite is true: The more we share frustrations, the more we further activate an interconnected anger system in the brain. We're building up steam rather than releasing it. We are causing our own stress!

And the opposite is true as well.

Fifteen years ago, Nadia took a long look at herself and decided to emulate her colleague, who bore up under hardship with poise, refused to speak unkindly behind their boss's back (no matter how deserved it was!), and chose to focus on the positives of the job. That process changed Nadia into someone who can now handle the most difficult clients in the country with grace. Sisters, as we go through that same process, our stress will dissipate, and praise will come naturally. Let's resolve to move forward for the sake of those around us—and for ourselves.

Reflect

What is most likely to cause discontent to arise in you? Going forward, what one habit would most change frustration to joy?

Notes

_____

_____

_____

_____

_____

_____

_____

_____

_____

"ONE OF THE BEAUTIFUL
THINGS ABOUT KINDNESS
IS THAT IT CHANGES YOUR
HEART TOWARD THE OTHER
PERSON SO THAT YOU WANT
TO KEEP BEING KIND."

— Shaunti Feldhahn,
*The Kindness Challenge:
Thirty Days to Improve Any Relationship*

Anyone who listens to my teaching and follows it is wise, like a
person who builds a house on solid rock. Though the rain comes
in torrents and the floodwaters rise and the winds beat against
that house, it won't collapse because it is built on bedrock.
— *Matthew 7:24-25*

Peace in the Storm

As soon as you finish this journey to finding rest and peace, the enemy is going to try all sorts of things to jar you out of it. You may have already seen him at work, in fact. He hates the children of God and loves whipping up storms to cause fear, worry, anxiety, stress—pretty much the opposite of rest.

Friends, let's not be caught unaware. Let's be wise and watchful. Over the next few weeks, when you see communication going sideways with your husband or boyfriend, see it for what it is. When you find yourself getting uncharacteristically irritated with your mother-in-law's political opinions, see it for what it is. If your paycheck isn't as big as you expected, you get sick, your kids cop an attitude, your colleague quits and leaves you with the entire planning project, and your hot water heater floods the basement—all in the same week—recognize the hand of the evil one at work.

In all these things, refuse to take the bait.

Jesus says there is one sure way to have peace in these storms: listen to His teaching and follow it, even when you absolutely do not feel

like it. Trust God with your financial or health situation. Respond with kindness to your kids and your coworkers. Maintain patience, good humor, and self-control as you figure out what to do about the moldy basement and lack of hot water in the house.

As you do, you will become like the house in the hurricane that is built on bedrock. You will not be shaken by the torrents, floodwaters, and winds of life. You can't change the force or trajectory of the storm, but you can change everything about how you experience it.

Friends, storms will come. Whether the storms are the enemy's attack to distract you from finding rest, the result of living in a broken world, or simply the consequence of your own imperfect choices, storms will come. And in those moments of irritation, anger, worry, or fear, it is so easy to forget everything Jesus asks of us.

Let's think ahead and ensure that does not happen. Let's pray that we see the lure of building on sand and turn away from it. That we cling to the Rock that is higher than we are—the Rock who wants us to build on Him alone.

Reflect

What types of storms might you face in the days and weeks ahead?
How can you be prepared to follow Jesus' teaching and stand firm
on the Rock in those storms, so that you can have peace?

Notes

_____

_____

_____

_____

_____

_____

_____

"LOWER YOUR
EXPECTATIONS OF
EARTH. THIS ISN'T
HEAVEN, SO DON'T
EXPECT IT TO BE."

— Max Lucado

Under his direction, the whole body is fitted together perfectly,
and each part in its own special way helps the other parts, so
that the whole body is healthy and growing and full of love.
— Ephesians 4:16, TLB

We are All in Ministry

Friends, as we wrap up our days together, let's tackle one final question: why does finding rest matter? We have spent sixty days looking at crucial factors that go into becoming women who are able to rest in Him. And He wants us to.

But why?

Remember how we are actually underground espionage agents for God's Kingdom (Day 12)? We are called to find rest not just for ourselves, but because it is a necessary foundation for the ministry calling God has for us.

No matter who you are or where you live, whether you are a stay-at-home mom, clerk at the corner store, or manager at a skyscraper downtown, you are in ministry. You may not have gone to seminary, you may not have a certificate of ordination on your wall, but you are a minister. You will come in contact with people your pastor will never meet. You will have opportunities to serve and love neighbors, colleagues, and friends that your women's ministry director never will.

Our lives feel stretched and disconnected when we run from task to task, role to role, trying to be "a good mom," "an effective

saleswoman," "a good small group leader," and "an attentive wife." It is as if we take off one work uniform and put on the next . . . and the next . . . and the next.

That all changes when we realize: I don't have four or five or ten roles—I have one: To be a minister of God's love and grace to everyone I meet.

One of the special things about the Graduate Christian Fellowship group at Harvard was the unique graduation-related ceremony we had before the regular commencement. It was called "The Ordination to Daily Work." Just as pastors are ordained, we were ceremoniously sent out for ministry in daily work and life. It served as a powerful, overt reminder that whether we were becoming an accountant, a doctor, or a Wall Street analyst, we were entering the mission field. As I headed to work on Wall Street, I was very aware that that wasn't my only (or even my main) job. My real job was to be a reflection of God's love and light no matter where I was or what I was doing.

Friends, ask the Lord to show you all the ways you are in ministry. You won't be as exhausted, frustrated, or stressed by your job when you see the opportunity to come alongside a colleague during a difficult time. You won't be as beaten down when you realize that you are the one the bosses can rely on to do your work with honesty and integrity. You won't be as irritated with your little one's constant demands when you see this tiring season as a brief moment to invest powerfully in his or her whole life ahead.

Not long ago on a Christian radio station, a host asked a female caller, "What's your occupation?" The woman responded: "I'm a disciple of Jesus Christ, but right now he has me disguised as a press operator." What a great response! This woman knows that her primary role in life is that of a disciple living out her ministry wherever she is called.

Take the yoke of Jesus, see that it is light, find peace and rest in doing things His way—and you'll see Jesus guiding you to minister that same peace to many others who deeply need it.

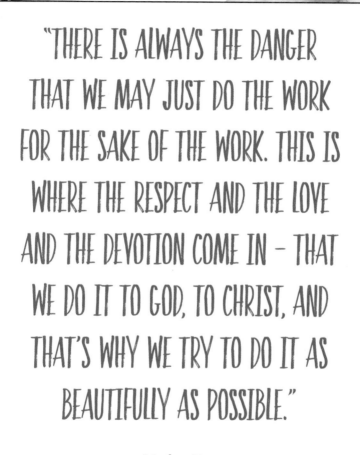

"THERE IS ALWAYS THE DANGER THAT WE MAY JUST DO THE WORK FOR THE SAKE OF THE WORK. THIS IS WHERE THE RESPECT AND THE LOVE AND THE DEVOTION COME IN – THAT WE DO IT TO GOD, TO CHRIST, AND THAT'S WHY WE TRY TO DO IT AS BEAUTIFULLY AS POSSIBLE."

— Mother Teresa

Questions to Consider for the Days Ahead

Thinking back on all God has shown you in the last few months, what are the two or three main areas in which you have most grown in your ability to find rest? How are you finding rest in ways you were not before?

_____

_____

_____

_____

What specific habits have you already built, that are important to keep intact? How can you be sure to do so?

_____

_____

_____

_____

_____

Where are the main areas of ministry—near or far—to
which God has deployed you for the months ahead?

What two or three specific changes do you feel God is calling
you to make going forward that will help you be better rested
and equipped for your specific areas of ministry?

Finally, what can you give thanks for, that God has done or given you in your life? Make a long list—and come back to it in the weeks and months ahead, whenever you need to fix your eyes on Jesus.

"COURAGE, DEAR HEART."

— C.S. Lewis

The Voyage of The Dawn Treader

With My Thanks...

There are a lot of amazing individuals who probably need to "find rest" themselves after pouring their energy into this project!

Most importantly, I'm so honored to partner on the first iDisciple publishing project. To David Henriksen, Kobus Johnsen, Melissa Sladky, Ryn Tomlinson, Alex Ritchey, Kamilah Benjamin and many others: I'm blessed to work with such incredibly talented people who are using their gifts for the Kingdom. Here's to many other projects and cups of caramel vanilla coffee.

To Nancy Taylor, our fantastic editor: Thank you for somehow miraculously taking my wordy pieces and trimming them into something coherent and focused. You're amazing. Thanks also to Cinara Lothamer who took on the challenge of finding and sourcing many of the quotes.

To our outstanding artists, Christelle Van Rensburg and Annabelle Grobler: I'm in awe of the gift God has given you. Thank you for visually bringing us into the beauty of God's rest.

To Nancy DeMoss Wolgemuth: thank you for the beautiful Foreword, and your encouragement over so many years.

And to my amazing team . . . where do I begin? First, Charlyn Elliott and Katie Phillips: you two are rock stars. There is no way I can adequately thank you for how you came alongside this project. You helped me think through the topics, searched the Scriptures with me, wrote drafts of so many days, and kept me on track with deadlines (as much as you could, that is!). You encouraged me to find rest myself, and held up my arms when I couldn't hold up my own. This devo wouldn't exist without you.

To the others who helped with so many of the drafts; Linda Crews, Karen Bray, Dixie Walker, Cathy Kidd, and Brittany Good. Thank you for the many hours you poured into this project, and for helping me think through and flesh out what needed to be said. A special thank you also to my other team members: Caroline Niziol, Theresa Colquitt, and Naomi Duncan, who kept the ministry running while Charlyn and I were locked in meetings with iDisciple, managing the process, or writing. I'm very, very grateful for all you brilliant ladies.

Finally, to Jeff and two amazing kids: thank you for taking everything else off my shoulders while I was working on this project, for showing me constant love and encouragement, and for giving me the greatest possible motivation to set it all aside and find rest, downtime, and family movie nights. I love you all so much. To our prayer team: As always, we are so grateful to you for doing the real work. And ultimately, to our heavenly Father: there really are no words that can express my awe at your goodness. May you take this simple offering and use it for your glory.

— Shaunti Feldhahn

Sources

DAY 1 — A.W. Tozer quote from https://www.goodreads.com/quotes/1346489-when-i-understand-that-everything-happening-to-me-is-to

DAY 2 — Phillips Brooks quote from http://www.art-quotes.com/auth_search.php?authid=2486#.Wen_e9N96T8

DAY 3 — Brene Brown, *The Gifts of Imperfection: Let Go of Who You Think You're Supposed to Be and Embrace Who You Are* (Hazelden Publishing. Kindle Edition) p.102.

DAY 4 — Mother Teresa quote from https://www.brainyquote.com/quotes/quotes/m/mothertere164357.html

DAY 5 — Ralph Waldo Emerson quote from https://www.brainyquote.com/quotes/ralph_waldo_emerson_385779

DAY 6 — John Lennox quopte from http://www.azquotes.com/quote/1288487

DAY 7 — Dr. Jack Hyles quote from http://www.jackhyles.com/jackhylesquotes.html

DAY 8 — Billy Graham quote from https://www.goodreads.com/quotes/148871-i-ve-read-the-last-page-of-the-bible-it-s-all

DAY 9 — Mother Teresa quote from https://www.brainyquote.com/quotes/quotes/m/mothertere107846.html

DAY 10 — Marcus Tullius Cicero quote from https://www.brainyquote.com/quotes/quotes/m/marcustull122152.html

DAY 11 — Tim Keller, *Walking with God through Pain and Suffering.*

DAY 12 — Shaunti Feldhahn, *The Life Ready Woman: Thriving in a Do-It-All World* (no url, from the author's book, p.27)

DAY 13 — Marcus Aurelius quote from https://simplereminders. com/20140922043503.html

DAY 14 — Louie Giglio quote from http://www.hearitfirst.com/news/21-great- louie-giglio-quotes

DAY 15 — Aesop quote from https://www.brainyquote.com/quotes/quotes/a/ aesop109734.html

DAY 16 — Maria Shriver, *Ten Things I Wish I'd Known – Before I Went Out Into the Real World*

DAY 17 — Will Rogers quote from https://www.goodreads.com/quotes/605563- good- judgment-comes-from-experience-and-a-lot-of-that

DAY 18 — Saint Augustine quote from https://www.scrapbook.com/quotes/ doc/29855.html

DAY 19 — Lysa TerKeurst, *The Best Yes: Making Wise Decisions in the Midst of Endless Demands* (Thomas Nelson. Kindle Edition) p. 189.

DAY 20 — William Shakespeare quote from https://www.forbes.com/quotes/ 10237/

DAY 21 — Ovid quote from https://www.goodreads.com/quotes/183226-take- rest-a-field-that-has-rested-gives-a-beautiful

DAY 22 — Francis Chan quote from http://quoteprism.net/quote/francis- chan/568691-our-culture-is-all-about-shallow-relationships-but?src= stop-quotes

DAY 23 — Winston S. Churchill quote from https://www.goodreads.com/quotes /3270-success-is-not-final-failure-is-not-fatal-it-is

Sources

DAY 24 — Louie Giglio quote from https://www.pinterest.com/pin/
362047257522472024

DAY 25 — Author Unknown quote from https://inspirationalquotes4life.
wordpress.com/2014/08/06/when-god-pushes-you-to-the-edge-of-
difficulty-trust-him-fully-because-two-things-can-happen-either-
hell-catch-you-when-you-fall-or-he-will-teach-you-how-to-fly/

DAY 26 — C.S. Lewis quote from https://www.goodreads.com/quotes/81968-
there-is-but-one-good-that-is-god-everything-else

DAY 27 — Shaunti Feldhahn, *The Life Ready Woman: Thriving in a
Do-It-All World*

DAY 28 — Saint Augustine quote from https://www.brainyquote.com/quotes/
quotes/s/saintaugus384531.html?src=t_resentment

DAY 29 — Steven Furtick quote from http://quozio.com/quote/710fd41f#!t=1010

DAY 30 — Nancy DeMoss, *The Quiet Place: Daily Devotional Readings,* July 13

DAY 31 — Brené Brown quote from https://quotefancy.com/quote/777887/Bren-
Brown-We-are-a-culture-of-people-who-ve-bought-into-the-idea-
that-if-we-stay-busy

DAY 32 — Lysa TerKeurst, *Unglued: Making Wise Choices in the
Midst of Raw Emotions* (*Thomas Nelson. Kindle* Edition) 185-186.

DAY 33 — Beth Moore quote from https://www.goodreads.com/quotes/229400-
we-re-going-to-have-to-let-truth-scream-louder-to

DAY 34 — Priscilla Shirer quote from https://www.pinterest.com/pin/
162481499037307566

DAY 35 — Jennifer Rothschild quote from https://www.pinterest.com/pin/
8444318028746858

DAY 36 — Mike Foster's tweet from :https://twitter.com/MikeFoster/status/
441363820066664449

DAY 37 — Amy Carmichael quote from http://www.azquotes.com/quote/424437

DAY 38 — Priscilla Shirer quote from https://www.pinterest.com/pin/
197876977353032639

DAY 39 — Tony Gaskins quote from https://twitter.com/tonygaskins/status/
314388211726168065?lang=en

DAY 40 — Shaunti Feldhahn, *For Women Only: What You Need to Know About
the Inner Lives of Men*

DAY 41 — Author Unknown quote referenced in the movie *God's Not Dead 2*
http://www.imdb.com/title/tt4824308/quotes

DAY 42 — John Piper quote from https://www.goodreads.com/quotes/701102-
faith-is-born-and-sustained-by-the-word-of-god

DAY 43 — Kathi Lipp, *Overwhelmed: How to Quiet the Chaos and
Restore Your Sanity,* (http://www.laurengaskillinspires.com/hope-
feeling-overwhelmed-kathi-lipp/)

DAY 44 — Lysa TerKeurst, *The Best Yes: Making Wise Decisions in
the Midst of Endless Demands,* (Thomas Nelson. Kindle Edition) p. 5.

DAY 45 — Thomas Jefferson quote form https://www.brainyquote.com/quotes/
quotes/t/thomasjeff101007.html

Sources

DAY 46 — Michele Cushatt quote from https://www.pinterest.com/pin/204280533076999674

DAY 47 — Francis of Assisi quote from https://www.brainyquote.cquotes/f/francisofa389169.html

DAY 48 — Corrie Ten Boom quote from https://www.brainyquote.com/quotes/quotes/c/corrietenb381184.html

DAY 49 — Max Lucado quote from https://www.brainyquote.com/quotes/quotes/m/maxlucado543039.html

DAY 50 — John Piper, *Desiring God: Meditations of a Christian Hedonist* (https://www.goodreads.com/quotes/793633-god-is-most-glorified-when-you-are-most-satisfied-in)

DAY 51 — William Shakespeare quote from *Romeo and Juliet* (modern translation) Act 1, Scene 4, page 2 http://nfs.sparknotes.com/romeojuliet/page_50.html

DAY 52 — Mary Ann Evans quote from (pen name: George Eliot), *Middlemarch* https://www.goodreads.com/quotes/2801-but-the-effect-of-her-being-on-those-around-her

DAY 53 — Paul Tripp quote from *Jonah* video Bible Study http://store.gotothehub.com/paul-tripps-jonah-video-bible-study-you-cant-outrun-grace-dvd-study-guide/

DAY 54 — Dr. Hans Selye quote from https://www.brainyquote.com/quotes/hans_selye_381380

DAY 55 — Charles Spurgeon quote from https://www.goodreads.com/quotes/815088-i-have-now-concentrated-all-my-prayers-into-one-and

DAY 56 — Martin Luther King, Jr. quote from https://www.brainyquote.com/
quotes/quotes/m/martinluth110082.html?src=t_love

DAY 57 — John Galsworthy quote from https://www.brainyquote.com/quotes/
quotes/j/johngalswo380209.html

DAY 58 — Shaunti Feldhahn, *The Kindness Challenge: Thirty Days to Improve
Any Relationship,* p.152.

DAY 59 — Max Lucado quote from https://www.goodreads.com/quotes/28453-
lower-your-expectations-of-earth-this-isn-t-heaven-so-don-t

DAY 60 — Mother Teresa quote from https://www.values.com/inspirational-
quotes/4430-there-is-always-the-danger-that-we-may-just-do

END QUOTE — C.S. Lewis, *The Voyage of the Dawn Treader*
https://www.goodreads.com/quotes/159530-but-no-one-except-lucy-
knew-that-as-it-circled

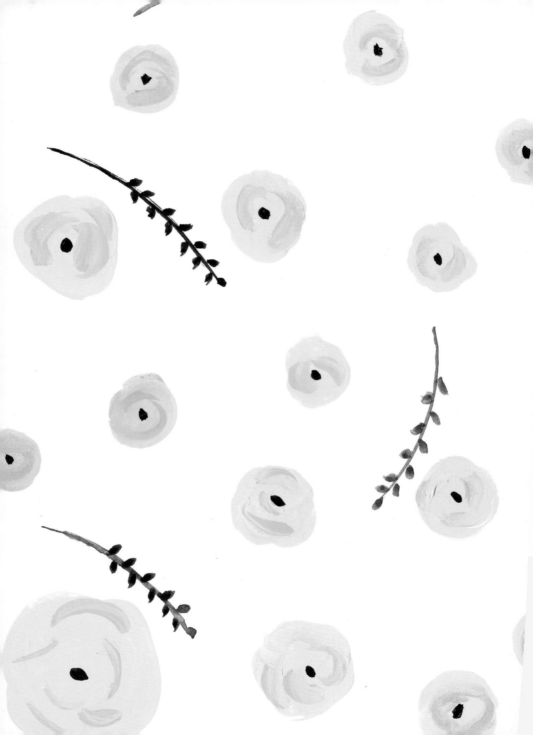